William Shakespeare's

Twelfth Night

Text by
Frederic Kolman
(M.A., Rutgers University)
Foreign Language Department
Louis D. Brandeis High School
New York, New York

Illustrations by
Lidia Nesterova

Research & Education Association

MAXnotes® for
TWELFTH NIGHT

Copyright © 1996 by Research & Education
Association. All rights reserved. No part of this
book may be reproduced in any form without
permission of the publisher.

Printed in the United States of America

Library of Congress Catalog Card Number 96-67444

International Standard Book Number 0-87891-055-7

MAXnotes® is a registered trademark of
Research & Education Association, Piscataway, New Jersey 08854

What **MAXnotes®** *Will Do for You*

This book is intended to help you absorb the essential contents and features of William Shakespeare's *Twelfth Night* and to help you gain a thorough understanding of the work. The book has been designed to do this more quickly and effectively than any other study guide.

For best results, this **MAXnotes** book should be used as a companion to the actual work, not instead of it. The interaction between the two will greatly benefit you.

To help you in your studies, this book presents the most up-to-date interpretations of every section of the actual work, followed by questions and fully explained answers that will enable you to analyze the material critically. The questions also will help you to test your understanding of the work and will prepare you for discussions and exams.

Meaningful illustrations are included to further enhance your understanding and enjoyment of the literary work. The illustrations are designed to place you into the mood and spirit of the work's settings.

The **MAXnotes** also include summaries, character lists, explanations of plot, and section-by-section analyses. A biography of the author and discussion of the work's historical context will help you put this literary piece into the proper perspective of what is taking place.

The use of this study guide will save you the hours of preparation time that would ordinarily be required to arrive at a complete grasp of this work of literature. You will be well prepared for classroom discussions, homework, and exams. The guidelines that are included for writing papers and reports on various topics will prepare you for any added work which may be assigned.

The **MAXnotes** will take your grades "to the max."

Dr. Max Fogiel
Program Director

Contents

Each scene includes List of Characters, Summary, Analysis, Study Questions and Answers, and Suggested Essay Topics.

SECTION ONE

Introduction

The Life and Work of William Shakespeare

The details of William Shakespeare's life are sketchy, mostly mere surmise based upon court or other clerical records. His parents, John and Mary (Arden), were married about 1557; she was of the landed gentry, and he was a yeoman—a glover and commodities merchant. By 1568, John had risen through the ranks of town government and held the position of high bailiff, which was a position similar to mayor. William, the eldest son and the third of eight children, was born in 1564, probably on April 23, several days before his baptism on April 26 in Stratford-upon-Avon. Shakespeare is also believed to have died on the same date—April 23—in 1616.

It is believed that William attended the local grammar school in Stratford where his parents lived, and that he studied primarily Latin, rhetoric, logic, and literature. Shakespeare probably left school at age 15, which was the norm, to take a job, especially since this was the period of his father's financial difficulty. At age 18 (1582), William married Anne Hathaway, a local farmer's daughter who was eight years his senior. Their first daughter (Susanna) was born six months later (1583), and twins Judith and Hamnet were born in 1585.

Shakespeare's life can be divided into three periods: the first 20 years in Stratford, which include his schooling, early marriage, and fatherhood; the next 25 years as an actor and playwright in London; and the last five in retirement in Stratford where he enjoyed moderate wealth gained from his theatrical successes. The years linking the first two periods are marked by a lack of information about Shakespeare, and are often referred to as the "dark years."

At some point during the "dark years," Shakespeare began his career with a London theatrical company, perhaps in 1589, for he was already an actor and playwright of some note by 1592. Shakespeare apparently wrote and acted for numerous theatrical companies, including Pembroke's Men, and Strange's Men, which later became the Chamberlain's Men, with whom he remained for the rest of his career.

In 1592, the Plague closed the theaters for about two years, and Shakespeare turned to writing book-length narrative poetry. Most notable were *Venus and Adonis* and *The Rape of Lucrece*, both of which were dedicated to the Earl of Southampton, whom scholars accept as Shakespeare's friend and benefactor despite a lack of documentation. During this same period, Shakespeare was writing his sonnets, which are more likely signs of the time's fashion rather than actual love poems detailing any particular relationship. He returned to playwriting when theaters reopened in 1594, and did not continue to write poetry. His sonnets were published without his consent in 1609, shortly before his retirement.

Amid all of his success, Shakespeare suffered the loss of his only son, Hamnet, who died in 1596 at the age of 11. But Shakespeare's career continued unabated, and in London in 1599, he became one of the partners in the new Globe Theater, which was built by the Chamberlain's Men.

Shakespeare wrote very little after 1612, which was the year he completed *Henry VIII*. It was during a performance of this play in 1613 that the Globe caught fire and burned to the ground. Sometime between 1610 and 1613, Shakespeare returned to Stratford, where he owned a large house and property, to spend his remaining years with his family.

William Shakespeare died on April 23, 1616, and was buried two days later in the chancel of Holy Trinity Church, where he had been baptized exactly 52 years earlier. His literary legacy included 37 plays, 154 sonnets, and five major poems.

Incredibly, most of Shakespeare's plays had never been published in anything except pamphlet form, and were simply extant as acting scripts stored at the Globe. Theater scripts were not regarded as literary works of art, but only the basis for the performance. Plays were simply a popular form of entertainment for all layers of society in Shakespeare's time. Only the efforts of two of Shakespeare's company, John Heminges and Henry Condell, preserved his 36 plays (minus *Pericles*, the thirty-seventh).

Shakespeare's Language

Shakespeare's language can create a strong pang of intimidation, even fear, in a large number of modern-day readers. Fortunately, however, this need not be the case. All that is needed to master the art of reading Shakespeare is to practice the techniques of unraveling uncommonly-structured sentences and to become familiar with the poetic use of uncommon words. We must realize that during the 400-year span between Shakespeare's time and our own, both the way we live and speak has changed. Although most of his vocabulary is in use today, some of it is obsolete, and what may be most confusing is that some of his words are used today, but with slightly different or totally different meanings. On the stage, actors readily dissolve these language stumbling blocks. They study Shakespeare's dialogue and express it dramatically in word and in action so that its meaning is graphically enacted. If the reader studies Shakespeare's lines as an actor does, looking up and reflecting upon the meaning of unfamiliar words until real voice is discovered, he or she will suddenly experience the excitement, the depth and the sheer poetry of what these characters say.

Shakespeare's Sentences

In English, or any other language, the meaning of a sentence greatly depends upon where each word is placed in that sentence. "The child hurt the mother" and "The mother hurt the child" have opposite meanings, even though the words are the same, simply because the words are arranged differently. Because word position is so integral to English, the reader will find unfamiliar word arrangements confusing, even difficult to understand. Since Shakespeare's plays are poetic dramas, he often shifts from average word arrangements to the strikingly unusual so that the line will conform to the desired poetic rhythm. Often, too, Shakespeare employs unusual word order to afford a character his own specific style of speaking.

Today, English sentence structure follows a sequence of subject first, verb second, and an optional object third. Shakespeare, however, often places the verb before the subject, which reads, "Speaks he" rather than "He speaks." Solanio speaks with this inverted structure in *The Merchant of Venice* stating, "I should be still/ Plucking the grass to know where sits the wind" (Bevington edition, I, i, ll.17-19), while today's standard English word order would have the clause at the end of this line read, "where the wind sits." "Wind" is the subject of this clause, and "sits" is the verb. Bassanio's words in Act Two also exemplify this inversion: "And in such eyes as ours appear not faults" (II, ii, l. 184). In our normal word order, we would say, "Faults do not appear in eyes such as ours," with "faults" as the subject in both Shakespeare's word order and ours.

Inversions like these are not troublesome, but when Shakespeare positions the predicate adjective or the object before the subject and verb, we are sometimes surprised. For example, rather than "I saw him," Shakespeare may use a structure such as "Him I saw." Similarly, "Cold the morning is" would be used for our "The morning is cold." Lady Macbeth demonstrates this inversion as she speaks of her husband: "Glamis thou art, and Cawdor, and shalt be/What thou art promised" (Macbeth, I, v, ll. 14-15). In current English word order, this quote would begin, "Thou art Glamis, and Cawdor."

In addition to inversions, Shakespeare purposefully keeps words apart that we generally keep together. To illustrate, consider Bassanio's humble admission in *The Merchant of Venice*: "I owe you much, and, like a wilful youth,/That which I owe is lost" (I, i, ll. 146-147). The phrase, "like a wilful youth," separates the regular sequence of "I owe you much" and "That which I owe is lost." To understand more clearly this type of passage, the reader could rearrange these word groups into our conventional order: I owe you much and I wasted what you gave me because I was young and impulsive. While these rearranged clauses will sound like normal English, and will be simpler to understand, they will no longer have the desired poetic rhythm, and the emphasis will now be on the wrong words.

As we read Shakespeare, we will find words that are separated by long, interruptive statements. Often subjects are separated from verbs, and verbs are separated from objects. These long interruptions can be used to give a character dimension or to add an element of suspense. For example, in *Romeo and Juliet* Benvolio describes both Romeo's moodiness and his own sensitive and thoughtful nature:

> I, measuring his affections by my own,
> Which then most sought, where most might not be found,
> Being one too many by my weary self,
> Pursu'd my humour, not pursuing his,
> And gladly shunn'd who gladly fled from me. (I, i, ll. 126-130)

In this passage, the subject "I" is distanced from its verb "Pursu'd." The long interruption serves to provide information which is integral to the plot. Another example, taken from *Hamlet*, is the ghost, Hamlet's father, who describes Hamlet's uncle, Claudius, as

> ...that incestuous, that adulterate beast,
> With witchcraft of his wit, with traitorous gifts—
> O wicked wit and gifts, that have the power
> So to seduce—won to his shameful lust
> The will of my most seeming virtuous queen. (I, v, ll. 43-47)

From this we learn that Prince Hamlet's mother is the victim of an evil seduction and deception. The delay between the subject, "beast," and the verb, "won," creates a moment of tension filled with the image of a cunning predator waiting for the right moment to spring into attack. This interruptive passage allows the play to unfold crucial information and thus to build the tension necessary to produce a riveting drama.

While at times these long delays are merely for decorative purposes, they are often used to narrate a particular situation or to enhance character development. As *Antony and Cleopatra* opens, an interruptive passage occurs in the first few lines. Although the delay is not lengthy, Philo's words vividly portray Antony's military prowess while they also reveal the immediate concern of the drama. Antony is distracted from his career, and is now focused on Cleopatra:

>   ...those goodly eyes,
> That o'er the files and musters of the war
> Have glow'd like plated Mars, now bend, now turn
> The office and devotion of their view
> Upon a tawny front.... (I, i, ll. 2-6)

Whereas Shakespeare sometimes heaps detail upon detail, his sentences are often elliptical, that is, they omit words we expect in written English sentences. In fact, we often do this in our spoken conversations. For instance, we say, "You see that?" when we really mean, "Did you see that?" Reading poetry or listening to lyrics in music conditions us to supply the omitted words and it makes us more comfortable reading this type of dialogue. Consider one passage in *The Merchant of Venice* where Antonio's friends ask him why he seems so sad and Solanio tells Antonio, "Why, then you are in love" (I, i, l. 46). When Antonio denies this, Solanio responds, "Not in love neither?" (I, i, l. 47). The word "you" is omitted but understood despite the confusing double negative.

In addition to leaving out words, Shakespeare often uses intentionally vague language, a strategy which taxes the reader's attentiveness. In *Antony and Cleopatra*, Cleopatra, upset that Antony is leaving for Rome after learning that his wife died in battle, convinces him to stay in Egypt:

> Sir, you and I must part, but that's not it:
> Sir you and I have lov'd, but there's not it;
> That you know well, something it is I would—
> O, my oblivion is a very Antony,
> And I am all forgotten. (I, iii, ll. 87-91, emphasis added)

In line 89, "...something it is I would" suggests that there is something that she would want to say, do, or have done. The intentional vagueness leaves us, and certainly Antony, to wonder. Though this sort of writing may appear lackadaisical for all that it leaves out, here the vagueness functions to portray Cleopatra as rhetorically sophisticated. Similarly, when asked what thing a crocodile is (meaning Antony himself who is being compared to a

crocodile), Antony slyly evades the question by giving a vague reply:

> It is shap'd, sir, like itself, and it is as broad as it hath
> breadth. It is just so high as it is, and moves with it own
> organs. It lives by that which nourisheth it, and, the
> elements once out of it, it transmigrates. (II, vii, ll. 43-46)

This kind of evasiveness, or doubletalk, occurs often in Shakespeare's writing and requires extra patience on the part of the reader.

Shakespeare's Words

As we read Shakespeare's plays, we will encounter uncommon
words. Many of these words are not in use today. As *Romeo and
Juliet* opens, we notice words like "shrift" (confession) and
"holidame" (a holy relic). Words like these should be explained in
notes to the text. Shakespeare also employs words which we still
use, though with different meaning. For example, in *The Merchant
of Venice* "caskets" refer to small, decorative chests for holding jew-
els. However, modern readers may think of a large cask instead of
the smaller, diminutive casket.

Another trouble modern readers will have with Shakespeare's
English is with words that are still in use today, but which mean
something different in Elizabethan use. In *The Merchant of Venice*,
Shakespeare uses the word "straight" (as in "straight away") where
we would say "immediately." Here, the modern reader is unlikely
to carry away the wrong message, however, since the modern
meaning will simply make no sense. In this case, textual notes will
clarify a phrase's meaning. To cite another example, in *Romeo and
Juliet*, after Mercutio dies, Romeo states that the "black fate on moe
days doth depend" (emphasis added). In this case, "depend" really
means "impend."

Shakespeare's Wordplay

All of Shakespeare's works exhibit his mastery of playing with
language and with such variety that many people have authored
entire books on this subject alone. Shakespeare's most frequently
used types of wordplay are common: metaphors, similes, synec-

doche and metonymy, personification, allusion, and puns. It is when Shakespeare violates the normal use of these devices, or rhetorical figures, that the language becomes confusing.

A metaphor is a comparison in which an object or idea is replaced by another object or idea with common attributes. For example, in *Macbeth* a murderer tells Macbeth that Banquo has been murdered, as directed, but that his son, Fleance, escaped, having witnessed his father's murder. Fleance, now a threat to Macbeth, is described as a serpent:

> There the grown serpent lies, the worm that's fled
> Hath nature that in time will venom breed,
> No teeth for the present. (III, iv, ll. 29-31, emphasis added)

Similes, on the other hand, compare objects or ideas while using the words "like" or "as." In *Romeo and Juliet,* Romeo tells Juliet that "Love goes toward love as schoolboys from their books" (II, ii, l. 156). Such similes often give way to more involved comparisons, "extended similes." For example, Juliet tells Romeo:

> 'Tis almost morning, I would have thee gone,
> And yet no farther than a wonton's bird,
> That lets it hop a little from his hand
> Like a poor prisoner in his twisted gyves,
> And with silken thread plucks it back again,
> So loving-jealous of his liberty.
> (II, ii, ll. 176-181, emphasis added)

An epic simile, a device borrowed from heroic poetry, is an extended simile that builds into an even more elaborate comparison. In *Macbeth*, Macbeth describes King Duncan's virtues with an angelic, celestial simile and then drives immediately into another simile that redirects us into a vision of warfare and destruction:

>   ...Besides this Duncan
> Hath borne his faculties so meek, hath been
> So clear in his great office, that his virtues
> Will plead like angels, trumpet-tongued, against

> The deep damnation of his taking-off;
> And pity, like a naked new-born babe,
> Striding the blast, or heaven's cherubim, horsed
> Upon the sightless couriers of the air,
> Shall blow the horrid deed in every eye,
> That tears shall drown the wind....
> (I, vii, ll. 16-25, emphasis added)

Shakespeare employs other devices, like synecdoche and metonymy, to achieve "verbal economy," or using one or two words to express more than one thought. Synecdoche is a figure of speech using a part for the whole. An example of synecdoche is using the word boards to imply a stage. Boards are only a small part of the materials that make up a stage, however, the term boards has become a colloquial synonym for stage. Metonymy is a figure of speech using the name of one thing for that of another which it is associated. An example of metonymy is using crown to mean the king (as used in the sentence "These lands belong to the crown"). Since a crown is associated with or an attribute of the king, the word crown has become a metonymy for the king. It is important to understand that every metonymy is a synecdoche, but not every synecdoche is a metonymy. This is rule is true because a metonymy must not only be a part of the root word, making a synecdoche, but also be a unique attribute of or associated with the root word.

Synecdoche and metonymy in Shakespeare's works is often very confusing to a new student because he creates uses for words that they usually do not perform. This technique is often complicated and yet very subtle, which makes it difficult of a new student to dissect and understand. An example of these devices in one of Shakespeare's plays can be found in *The Merchant of Venice* . In warning his daughter, Jessica, to ignore the Christian revelries in the streets below, Shylock says:

> Lock up my doors; and when you hear the drum
> And the vile squealing of the wry-necked fife,
> Clamber not you up to the casements then...
> (I, v, ll. 30-32)

The phrase of importance in this quote is "the wry-necked fife." When a reader examines this phrase it does not seem to make sense; a fife is a cylinder-shaped instrument, there is no part of it that can be called a neck. The phrase then must be taken to refer to the fife-player, who has to twist his or her neck to play the fife. Fife, therefore, is a synecdoche for fife-player, much as boards is for stage. The trouble with understanding this phrase is that "vile squealing" logically refers to the sound of the fife, not the fife-player, and the reader might be led to take fife as the instrument because of the parallel reference to "drum" in the previous line. The best solution to this quandary is that Shakespeare uses the word fife to refer to both the instrument and the player. Both the player and the instrument are needed to complete the wordplay in this phrase, which, though difficult to understand to new read-ers, cannot be seen as a flaw since Shakespeare manages to convey two meanings with one word. This remarkable example of synecdoche illuminates Shakespeare's mastery of "verbal economy."

Shakespeare also uses vivid and imagistic wordplay through personification, in which human capacities and behaviors are at-tributed to inanimate objects. Bassanio, in *The Merchant of Venice*, almost speechless when Portia promises to marry him and share all her worldly wealth, states "my blood speaks to you in my veins..." (III, ii, l. 176). How deeply he must feel since even his blood can speak. Similarly, Portia, learning of the penalty that Antonio must pay for defaulting on his debt, tells Salerio, "There are some shrewd contents in yond same paper/That steals the color from Bassanio's cheek" (III, ii, ll. 243-244).

Another important facet of Shakespeare's rhetorical repertoire is his use of allusion. An allusion is a reference to another author or to an historical figure or event. Very often Shakespeare alludes to the heroes and heroines of Ovid's *Metamorphoses*. For example, in Cymbeline an entire room is decorated with images illustrating the stories from this classical work, and the heroine, Imogen, has been reading from this text. Similarly, in *Titus Andronicus* charac-ters not only read directly from the *Metamorphoses*, but a subplot re-enacts one of the *Metamorphoses's* most famous stories, the rape and mutilation of Philomel.

Another way Shakespeare uses allusion is to drop names of mythological, historical and literary figures. In *The Taming of the Shrew*, for instance, Petruchio compares Katharina, the woman whom he is courting, to Diana (II, i, l. 55), the virgin goddess, in order to suggest that Katharina is a man-hater. At times, Shakespeare will allude to well-known figures without so much as mentioning their names. In *Twelfth Night*, for example, though the Duke and Valentine are ostensibly interested in Olivia, a rich countess, Shakespeare asks his audience to compare the Duke's emotional turmoil to the plight of Acteon, whom the goddess Diana transforms into a deer to be hunted and killed by Acteon's own dogs:

Duke: That instant was I turn'd into a hart,
           And my desires, like fell and cruel hounds,
           E'er since pursue me.
           [...]
Valentine: But like a cloistress she will veiled walk,
           And water once a day her chamber round....
           (I, i, l. 20 ff.)

Shakespeare's use of puns spotlights his exceptional wit. His comedies in particular are loaded with puns, usually of a sexual nature. Puns work through the ambiguity that results when multiple senses of a word are evoked; homophones often cause this sort of ambiguity. In *Antony and Cleopatra*, Enobarbus believes "there is mettle in death" (I, ii, l. 146), meaning that there is "courage" in death; at the same time, mettle suggests the homophone metal, referring to swords made of metal causing death. In early editions of Shakespeare's work there was no distinction made between the two words. Antony puns on the word "earing," (I, ii, ll. 112-114) meaning both plowing (as in rooting out weeds) and hearing: he angrily sends away a messenger, not wishing to hear the message from his wife, Fulvia: "...O then we bring forth weeds,/ when our quick minds lie still, and our ills told us/Is as our earing." If ill-natured news is planted in one's "hearing," it will render an "earing" (harvest) of ill-natured thoughts. A particularly clever pun, also in *Antony and Cleopatra*, stands out after Antony's troops have fought Octavius's men in Egypt: "We have beat him to his camp.

Run one before,/And let the queen know of our gests" (IV, viii, ll. 1-2). Here "gests" means deeds (in this case, deeds of battle); it is also a pun on "guests," as though Octavius' slain soldiers were to be guests when buried in Egypt.

One should note that Elizabethan pronunciation was in several cases different from our own. Thus, modern readers, especially Americans, will miss out on the many puns based on homophones. The textual notes will point up many of these "lost" puns, however.

Shakespeare's sexual innuendoes can be either clever or tedious depending upon the speaker and situation. The modern reader should recall that sexuality in Shakespeare's time was far more complex than in ours and that characters may refer to such things as masturbation and homosexual activity. Textual notes in some editions will point out these puns but rarely explain them. An example of a sexual pun or innuendo can be found in *The Merchant of Venice* when Portia and Nerissa are discussing Portia's past suitors using innuendo to tell of their sexual prowess:

Portia:	I pray thee, overname them, and as thou namest them, I will describe them, and according to my description level at my affection.
Nerrisa:	First, there is the Neapolitan prince.
Portia:	Ay, that's a colt indeed, for he doth nothing but talk of his horse, and he makes it a great appropriation to his own good parts that he can shoe him himself. I am much afeard my lady his mother played false with the smith.

(I, ii, ll. 35-45)

The "Neapolitan prince" is given a grade of an inexperienced youth when Portia describes him as a "colt." The prince is thought to be inexperienced because he did nothing but "talk of his horse" (a pun for his penis) and his other great attributes. Portia goes on to say that the prince boasted that he could "shoe him [his horse] himself," a possible pun meaning that the prince was very proud that he could masturbate. Finally, Portia makes an attack upon the prince's mother, saying that "my lady his mother played false with the smith," a pun to say his mother must have committed adultery with a blacksmith to give birth to such a vulgar man having an obsession with "shoeing his horse."

It is worth mentioning that Shakespeare gives the reader hints when his characters might be using puns and innuendoes. In *The Merchant of Venice*, Portia's lines are given in prose when she is joking, or engaged in bawdy conversations. Later on the reader will notice that Portia's lines are rhymed in poetry, such as when she is talking in court or to Bassanio. This is Shakespeare's way of letting the reader know when Portia is jesting and when she is serious.

Shakespeare's Dramatic Verse

Finally, the reader will notice that some lines are actually rhymed verse while others are in verse without rhyme; and much of Shakespeare's drama is in prose. Shakespeare usually has his lovers speak in the language of love poetry which uses rhymed couplets. The archetypal example of this comes, of course, from *Romeo and Juliet*:

> The grey-ey'd morn smiles on the frowning night,
> Check'ring the eastern clouds with streaks of light,
> And fleckled darkness like a drunkard reels
> From forth day's path and Titan's fiery wheels.
> (II, iii, ll. 1-4)

Here it is ironic that Friar Lawrence should speak these lines since he is not the one in love. He, therefore, appears buffoonish and out of touch with reality. Shakespeare often has his characters speak in rhymed verse to let the reader know that the character is acting in jest, and vice-versa.

Perhaps the majority of Shakespeare's lines are in blank verse, a form of poetry which does not use rhyme (hence the name blank) but still employs a rhythm native to the English language, iambic pentameter, where every second syllable in a line of ten syllables receives stress. Consider the following verses from *Hamlet*, and note the accents and the lack of end-rhyme:

The síngle ánd pecúliar lífe is bóund
With áll the stréngth and ármor óf the mínd
(III, iii, ll. 12-13)

The final syllable of these verses receives stress and is said to have a hard, or "strong," ending. A soft ending, also said to be "weak," receives no stress. In *The Tempest*, Shakespeare uses a soft ending to shape a verse that demonstrates through both sound (meter) and sense the capacity of the feminine to propagate:

and thén I lóv'd thee
And shów'd thee áll the quálitíes o' th' ísle,
The frésh spríngs, bríne-pits, bárren pláce and fértile.
(I, ii, ll. 338-40)

The first and third of these lines here have soft endings.

In general, Shakespeare saves blank verse for his characters of noble birth. Therefore, it is significant when his lofty characters speak in prose. Prose holds a special place in Shakespeare's dialogues; he uses it to represent the speech habits of the common people. Not only do lowly servants and common citizens speak in prose, but important, lower class figures also use this fun, at times ribald variety of speech. Though Shakespeare crafts some very ornate lines in verse, his prose can be equally daunting, for some of his characters may speechify and break into doubletalk in their attempts to show sophistication. A clever instance of this comes when the Third Citizen in Coriolanus refers to the people's paradoxical lack of power when they must elect Coriolanus as their new leader once Coriolanus has orated how he has courageously fought for them in battle:

We have power in ourselves to do it, but it is a power that we have no power to do; for if he show us his wounds and tell us his deeds, we are to put our tongues into those wounds and speak for them; so, if he tell us his noble deeds, we must also tell him our noble acceptance of them. Ingratitude is monstrous, and for the multitude to be ingrateful were to make a monster of the multitude,

of the which we, being members, should bring ourselves
to be monstrous members.
(II, ii, ll. 3-13)

Notice that this passage contains as many metaphors, hideous
though they be, as any other passage in Shakespeare's dramatic verse.

When reading Shakespeare, paying attention to characters who
suddenly break into rhymed verse, or who slip into prose after
speaking in blank verse, will heighten your awareness of a
character's mood and personal development. For instance, in
Antony and Cleopatra, the famous military leader Marcus Antony
usually speaks in blank verse, but also speaks in fits of prose (II, iii,
ll. 43-46) once his masculinity and authority have been questioned.
Similarly, in *Timon of Athens*, after the wealthy lord Timon aban-
dons the city of Athens to live in a cave, he harangues anyone whom
he encounters in prose (IV, iii, l. 331 ff.). In contrast, the reader
should wonder why the bestial Caliban in *The Tempest* speaks in
blank verse rather than in prose.

Implied Stage Action

When we read a Shakespearean play, we are reading a performance text. Actors interact through dialogue, but at the same time
these actors cry, gesticulate, throw tantrums, pick up daggers, and
compulsively wash murderous "blood" from their hands. Some of
the action that takes place on stage is explicitly stated in stage di-
rections. However, some of the stage activity is couched within the
dialogue itself. Attentiveness to these cues is important as one con-
ceives how to visualize the action. When Iago in *Othello* feigns concern for Cassio whom he himself has stabbed, he calls to the
surrounding men, "Come, come:/Lend me a light" (V, i, ll. 86-87). It
is almost sure that one of the actors involved will bring him a torch
or lantern. In the same play, Emilia, Desdemona's maidservant, asks
if she should fetch her lady's nightgown and Desdemona replies,
"No, unpin me here" (IV, iii, l. 37). In *Macbeth*, after killing Duncan,
Macbeth brings the murder weapon back with him. When he tells
his wife that he cannot return to the scene and place the daggers to
suggest that the king's guards murdered Duncan, she castigates him:

"Infirm of purpose/Give me the daggers. The sleeping and the dead are but as pictures" (II, ii, ll. 50-52). As she exits, it is easy to visualize Lady Macbeth grabbing the daggers from her husband.

For 400 years, readers have found it greatly satisfying to work with all aspects of Shakespeare's language—the implied stage action, word choice, sentence structure, and wordplay—until all aspects come to life. Just as seeing a fine performance of a Shakespearean play is exciting, staging the play in one's own mind's eye, and revisiting lines to enrich the sense of the action, will enhance one's appreciation of Shakespeare's extraordinary literary and dramatic achievements.

Historical Background

Although fifteenth-century England had been a time of grave civil unrest and violence, by the time Shakespeare achieved prominence during Elizabeth and James' reigns it was enjoying a period of socio-political security and respect for the arts. Queen Elizabeth's reign extended from 1558 until 1603, when she was succeeded by the Scottish King James. Shakespeare received the patronage of both monarchs during his career as a playwright.

Elizabeth's reign was not without its tensions. There was an intense religious climate in which the Queen had to act decisively. The religious tensions that existed during Elizabeth's reign continued during James' reign, when he was pitted against the Puritans. England had gone to war with Spain. In other foreign affairs, the Queen was moderate, practicing a prudent diplomatic neutrality. There were, however, several plots on her life.

There was also evidence of progress. The nation experienced a commercial revolution. Elizabeth's government instituted two important social measures: "the Statute of Artificers" and the "Poor Laws," both of which were aimed at helping the people displaced and hurt by changing conditions. Laws were passed to regulate the economy. Explorers started to venture into the unknown for riches and land. The machinery of government was transformed. The administrative style of government replaced the household form of leadership.

The Elizabethan Age was an age that made a great writer like Shakespeare and his contemporaries possible. It produced excellent drama; Marlowe's *Tamburlaine* and Jonson's *Every Man in His Humour* are two examples. Sir Philip Sidney and Edmund Spenser produced masterpieces during Elizabeth's reign. Shakespeare was in good company.

Shakespeare was well suited to the English Renaissance, with its new-found faith in the dignity and worth of the individual. Shakespeare profoundly understood human nature and provided us with some of the most imaginative character studies in drama. Shakespeare wrote for his company of players, known as the Lord Chamberlain's Men. He achieved considerable prosperity as a playwright. In addition to his artistic brilliance, Shakespeare wrote under the influence of the philosophy and effervescent spirit of the Elizabethan Age. Notably, we find the presence of the "Great Chain of Being," a view of life that started with Plato and Aristotle, in some of his plays. Furthermore, other ideas and social structures established in the Middle Ages still held sway during the early seventeenth century.

Shakespeare could display his universality and penetration in the public theater for his audience. His work, largely free of didactic and political motives, proved very entertaining.

The date of the composition of *Twelfth Night* is fixed around 1600. In using his creative powers on original sources, such as the Plautine *Gl'Ingannati* and Barnabe Rich's "Of Apolonius and Silla," Shakespeare was following a Renaissance tradition of working creatively with original situations. Shakespeare thus enjoyed artistic freedom and encouragement to produce a play like *Twelfth Night* for his audience, knowing that it would entertain viewers of all ages and status.

Master List of Characters

Orsino—*the Duke of Illyria, who is madly in love with Olivia.*

Olivia—*the countess with whom Orsino is in love and who rejects him.*

Curio—*one of the Duke's attendants.*

Valentine—*another gentlemen attending the Duke.*

Viola—*the female of a brother–sister pair of twins who enters Illyria disguised as Cesario and finds love.*

A Sea Captain—*a friend to Viola who comes ashore with her.*

Sir Toby Belch—*Olivia's uncle who drinks a lot and marries Maria.*

Maria—*Olivia's lady-in-waiting.*

Sir Andrew Aguecheek—*Sir Toby's friend who thinks he is a potential suitor for Olivia.*

Feste the Clown—*servant to Olivia who sings and provides entertainment.*

Malvolio—*steward to Olivia.*

Fabian—*another servant to Olivia.*

Antonio—*another sea captain who is friend to Viola and who comes ashore with Sebastian.*

Sebastian—*Viola's twin brother.*

First Officer—*officer in the service of the Duke.*

Second Officer—*also in the service of the Duke.*

A Priest—*marries Sebastian and Olivia.*

Musicians—*playing for Duke.*

Sailors—*come ashore with the Captain and Viola.*

Lords, Attendants

Summary of the Play

This is a play about love, placed in a festive atmosphere in which three couples are brought together happily. It opens with Orsino, the Duke of Illyria, expressing his deep love for the Countess Olivia. Meanwhile, the shipwrecked Viola disguises herself as a man and endeavors to enter the Duke's service. Although she has rejected his suit, the Duke then employs Viola, who takes the name of Cesario, to woo Olivia for him. Ironically, Cesario falls in love with the Duke, and Olivia falls in love with Cesario, who is really Viola disguised.

In the midst of this love triangle are the servants of Olivia's house and her Uncle Toby. The clown provides entertainment for the characters in both houses and speaks irreverently to them. He is the jester of the play. Maria, Olivia's woman, desires to seek revenge on Malvolio, Olivia's steward. To the delight of Sir Toby, Olivia's uncle, and his friend Sir Andrew, Maria comes up with a plot to drop love letters supposedly written by Olivia in Malvolio's path. When she does, they observe him, along with Fabian, another servant, as Malvolio falls for the bait. Believing that Olivia loves him, he makes a fool of himself.

The love plot moves along as Cesario goes to woo Olivia for the Duke. The second time that Cesario appears at Olivia's home Olivia openly declares her love for Cesario. All along, Sir Andrew has been nursing a hope to win Olivia's love. When he plans to give up on her, Sir Toby suggests that Sir Andrew fight with Cesario to impress Olivia. Cesario, however, refuses to fight.

In the meantime, Viola's brother, who is also shipwrecked, makes his way to safe lodging in Illyria with Antonio the sea captain. After the fight between Cesario and Sir Andrew begins, Antonio intervenes to save Cesario, whom he takes for Sebastian. But the Duke's officers promptly arrest Antonio for a past offense. Olivia later comes upon Sir Andrew and Sebastian wrangling at her house. Olivia, thinking Sebastian is Cesario, leads Sebastian to marriage in a nearby chapel.

The complications of identity are unraveled in the fifth act. Cesario finally reveals that he is Viola. Sebastian recognizes her as his sister. The Duke takes Viola up on her love offerings and proposes to her. Olivia assures Malvolio that she did not write the letter that so disturbed him. Sir Toby marries Maria in appreciation for her humiliating scheme.

Estimated Reading Time

You can read through *Twelfth Night* in about three and a half hours. But, when reading Shakespeare, you should plan to re-read at least one more time. When you read more carefully, paying attention to difficult words and Shakespeare's exquisite use of language, your reading time will necessarily increase. Your more careful reading may take about six hours.

Act I

Act I, Scene 1

New Characters:

Orsino: *the Duke of Illyria, who is madly in love with Olivia*

Curio: *one of the Duke's attendants*

Valentine: *another gentleman attending the Duke*

Summary

The play opens at the Duke's palace in Illyria. The Duke is lovesick, and so the first 15 lines express his powerful love for the Countess Olivia. He pours forth sweet words of passion for his love object.

He desires to have music feed his appetite for love. He feels at first that he can't get enough of the energizing "food of love," but abruptly urges the musicians to stop playing: "Enough, no more!"

Then, addressing the "spirit of love," he characterizes it as so broad a force that nothing can outdo or overcome it. Love is very, very powerful.

After this outpouring, one of the Duke's attendants, Curio, asks him if he plans to go hunting. But Orsino is in no mood for recreation; he is deeply in love. So his response is more than a mere "no." He says that his desire for Olivia has stronger control over him than anything else.

Valentine, another attendant, enters with words that the Duke

does want to listen to because they concern Olivia. Valentine informs the Duke of Olivia's mourning. She is grieving the loss of her dead brother and plans to stay in mourning for a long time. So, for her, love is out!

This news frustrates the Duke. He realizes that he will not achieve the object of his desire—at least, not yet. He recognizes that Olivia is full of love, but is channeling it in another direction, away from him. Still, his lover's hope does not lessen as long as he feels that love will awaken in Olivia.

Analysis

The first scene leads us instantly into the major theme of the play—love. Shakespeare, the skillful dramatist, wastes no time in developing it. In so doing, he uses poetic devices such as metaphor, simile, puns, and synesthesia to reveal the extraordinary nature of true love.

The poetry of the Duke's opening speech clearly conveys the power of his love for Olivia:

> If music be the food of love, play on,
> Give me excess of it, that, surfeiting,
> The appetite may sicken, and so die.

The Duke uses a physical metaphor of eating food to show how strong his experience of love is. He commands the musicians to overwhelm him with music, so that his lingering appetite for Olivia will die. He is totally wrapped up in his love for her.

Further on in the Duke's opening speech, he directly addresses the "spirit of love," using a falconry metaphor to indicate the depth of true love. One doesn't have to be a hunter to appreciate the thought he tries to convey. Consider that the sky is such a broad and spacious area and that falcons can reach great heights while flying. The power of the poetry here rests in comparing the experience of love with the falcon reaching its highest point in flight. It's a dizzying image. The bird reaches its highest point and then must come down to lower heights. Just as the falcon cannot outdistance the sky, so "nought" can overdo or overwhelm the power of love. All other forces and influences will "fall into abatement" if they try to overwhelm love.

The Duke has ample time to walk around his palace being in love, doing nothing else. This sense of stasis suggests that the Duke is illustrating true love in its intensity as it lasts. He is engaged in the process of loving; he has not entered into a relationship with Olivia or any other woman as yet.

Accordingly, it might be said that the Duke is "in love with love." But his speeches in Scene i; while exalting the business of love, also demonstrate that he knows his love object to be Olivia, a real, breathing person, and he makes an effort to win her.

The title of the play, *Twelfth Night*, orients the reader toward another element in the play, namely, that of the playful and festive atmosphere of the action. The Twelfth Night of Christmas was an occasion for merriment when a "Lord of Misrule" was appointed to direct the festivities. It is interesting that Shakespeare associated this particular holiday with the theme of love. In the festival running through the play, love plays an important part as the characters meet and pair off. Plots and affairs of love are entertaining to be involved in. The meaning of the subtitle, "What You Will," is not so apparent to the reader. It is spoken by Olivia at the end of Act I to Malvolio when she instructs him to get rid of Cesario, who's come to woo her for the Duke. The casualness of the phrase reflects her loose attitude toward the Duke's love. It points up the contrast between her feelings and those of the Duke. Feste, the Clown, will later emphasize this mundane level of love. It may also suggest a satire on the foibles of man.

Study Questions

1. What is the major theme of the play?

2. With whom is the Duke in love?

3. In what kinds of poetry does the Duke express his love?

4. Is it entirely true that the Duke is "in love with love"?

5. What type of metaphor does the Duke use when he addresses the "spirit of love"?

6. What is the subtitle of the play?

7. Toward what does the title *Twelfth Night* orient the reader?

8. What recreation does Curio ask the Duke about?

9. What is "Twelfth Night"?

10. What kind of part does love play in the festival atmosphere of the play?

Answers

1. Love is the major theme of the play.

2. The Duke is in love with Olivia.

3. The Duke's poetry contains metaphors, puns, synesthesia, and similes.

4. No, it is not completely true because the Duke is clearly in love with Olivia, a specific person.

5. He uses a metaphor drawn from falconry when he addresses the "spirit of love."

6. The subtitle of the play is "What You Will."

7. The title orients the reader toward the playful and festive atmosphere of the action.

8. Curio asks the Duke if he is going hunting.

9. "Twelfth Night" is a holiday and occasion for merriment.

10. Love plays an important part as the characters meet and pair off.

Suggested Essay Topics

1. Does the Duke's opening speech show praise for Olivia in particular or for the experience of love in general? Explain your answer by citing specific lines.

2. What kind of judgment would you make about the Duke's character based on his speech and behavior in the first scene? Discuss why you get this impression. Discuss either several specific qualities or one generalized personality trait.

Act I, Scene 2

New Characters:

Viola: *the female of a twin brother–sister pair, who enters Illyria disguised as Cesario and finds love*

A Sea Captain: *a friend to Viola who comes ashore with her*

Summary

The setting of this scene is appropriately away from the majestic atmosphere of the Duke's palace. We meet Viola and a captain on a seacoast. Viola's practical nature serves to complement the Duke's romantic character.

Shipwrecked, Viola asks the Captain and sailors where she is. The Captain tells her that they are in a region called "Illyria." Her brother, who had also been on the ship with her, is separated from them, which causes Viola to wonder if he has drowned. The Captain suggests that he may still be alive because he last saw him struggling to stay afloat.

The Captain was born and raised in Illyria, and he knows about the Duke's courtship with Olivia. The Captain relates Olivia's disinclination to accept Orsino's pledge, as he has heard from gossip.

Upon hearing this, Viola is moved to serve Olivia. But the Captain tells her that that is impossible. Olivia has closed herself off to any new relationships while she deeply mourns the loss of her brother.

Viola quickly gets another idea. She decides to serve the Duke instead, as his eunuch. Since she is a woman, that plan will require a disguise: "Conceal me what I am." This plan is very practical, for it utilizes a disguise. Viola claims to have a purpose in assuming a disguise, but, at this point, it is not clear exactly what she wants to achieve. She even says, "What else may hap, to time I will commit."

Analysis

This scene shifts the thematic emphasis to a practical, commonsense aspect of love. In so doing, Shakespeare is implying that there's more to love than mere poetry. It's all right to put one's

loved one up on a pedestal, but it also becomes necessary to find a way to get her down and together with the wooer. Valentine, the Duke's servant, had only gone to Olivia to report the Duke's love for her and obtain a favorable reply. Viola represents a viable plan of action to bring the two together in love. Her offerings of money to the Captain, for example, symbolize this practical side to her character. Money is a tool and a means to an end. Viola is well aware that money represents a way to get people to do what she wants.

The disguise plan has been used a lot in Shakespeare's plays. Here, as in *Measure for Measure* and *As You Like It*, a noble character puts on a mask in order to influence the behavior of other characters. Since Viola desires to serve the Duke, her goal may be to help make the love match a reality for him.

Relevant to her noble motivation is Viola's stating of a significant Shakespearean theme, that is, appearances versus the reality underlying them. Shakespeare knew all too well that appearances can be deceiving. People seem other than what they are in order to deceive or hurt other people. Viola comments perceptively on the Captain's true character. He is authentic and can be trusted. Her valuing of an authentic character implies that her own motivation is for the Duke's benefit.

Viola repeats the music image of the first scene. True to her character as we've seen it thus far, she has in mind a specific practical use for music. She plans to "speak to him in many sorts of music." Clearly, Viola wants to get on the Duke's good side and help him. So, she will use music to do so. Notice the active/passive contrast of each character's use of music. Whereas the Duke passively requests that his musicians play music so it will fill him to overflow, Viola contemplates the active use of music to get into the good graces of the Duke.

Study Questions

1. Where do we first meet Viola?

2. What happened to Viola's brother?

3. What kind of nature does Viola have?

4. What does Shakespeare imply about love in his shift of thematic emphasis?

5. What device does Viola use to get into the Duke's service?

6. Is it clear what Viola wants to achieve in the Duke's service?

7. How does Shakespeare symbolize Viola's practical side?

8. Is *Twelfth Night* the only play that involves a character putting on a disguise?

9. What other significant Shakespearean theme does Viola state?

10. What image that the Duke employs does Viola also use?

Answers

1. We first meet Viola on a seacoast.

2. He was separated from Viola when the ship sank.

3. Viola has a practical nature.

4. Shakespeare implies that there's more to love than mere poetry.

5. Viola uses the disguise device to get into the Duke's service.

6. No, it is not clear as yet what Viola's specific goal is.

7. Shakespeare symbolizes Viola's practical side by having her offer money in payment for favors to her.

8. No, Shakespeare has used disguised characters in other plays.

9. Viola states the theme of "appearances versus reality."

10. Viola repeats the music image of the first scene.

Suggested Essay Topics

1. Viola comments on the deceptiveness of appearances. People aren't always what they seem to be. Why do you think this theme would be significant in a play that deals with love? Cite evidence from the play to support your answer.

2. Why does the love object have to come down from the altar of the lover's worship? Why, that is, can't the Duke keep praising Olivia forever? How does Viola make it clear that there's more to being in love than just poetry? Make sure you present your topic sentences clearly in the essay.

Act I, Scene 3

New Characters:

Sir Toby Belch: *Olivia's uncle, who drinks a lot*

Maria: *Olivia's lady-in-waiting*

Sir Andrew Aguecheek: *Sir Toby's friend, who thinks he is a potential suitor for Olivia*

Summary

This scene is set in Olivia's house, but we do not as yet meet Olivia. She is in extended mourning. Sir Toby, her uncle, opens with a question about Olivia. He is talking to Maria, Olivia's lady-in-waiting, who responds with a complaint about Toby's late carousing.

Maria refers to Sir Toby's friend, Sir Andrew, as a fool. She heard that Sir Toby had brought him to the house to woo Olivia. Sir Toby, on the other hand, praises the many virtues his friend possesses. He is handsome, has a good income, and speaks several languages. Furthermore, they are drinking buddies.

When Sir Andrew enters, Sir Toby immediately urges him on Maria, "board her, woo her, assail her," though Sir Andrew misunderstands him at first. As Sir Toby's meaning dawns on him, he asserts that he wouldn't do such a thing in Olivia's house.

Before departing, Maria invites Sir Andrew for a drink. Sir Toby realizes that her invitation was made in a joking manner, and he engages Sir Andrew in a playful conversation. Sir Andrew talks of leaving, having lost hope of winning Olivia's love. He believes the Count Orsino has a much better chance for her than he does. Nonetheless, Sir Toby reassures him that his chances are

still good because Orsino is not the kind of man Olivia is looking for. This reassurance encourages Sir Andrew to stay a month longer.

So, continuing their conversation together, Sir Toby questions his friend's dancing ability. Sir Andrew says that he's quite a capable dancer. They then plan to go partying together.

Analysis

The characters of Maria and Sir Toby put us in touch with a lower class of people in Illyria; that is, they do not belong to the aristocracy as do Orsino and Olivia. This is a play for all kinds of people; love is for everyone. The disguise trick suggests this notion. It doesn't matter what your financial or social status is in love because true love does not play favorites. That is why Sir Andrew and Malvolio can entertain hopes of winning Olivia's love. Love is an experience that occurs between two human beings. A disguise can prove this statement because if you can conceal who or what you truly are, then it follows that it doesn't matter what your real identity is. Love can blossom. All is fair in love.

A note of competition enters the play in this scene. Sir Toby believes Sir Andrew to be a proper suitor for his niece. Despite his praise, however, the scene leaves us with the impression that Sir Andrew may not be so appropriate. Maria, for one, knocks him. By suggesting Sir Andrew for Olivia—in the light of his iffy status—Shakespeare asserts the universality of his love theme.

Beyond that, these characters illustrate the party-and-fun atmosphere, as implied in the title's holiday. They drink, dance, and flirt with the ladies, everything one would expect at a wild, exciting festival. There's a lighthearted playfulness all through the play; Sir Toby and Andrew seem to keep the celebration going. Their roles may be to suggest that liveliness and fun should surround the process of falling in love.

Notice how Shakespeare uses the language to reveal Sir Toby's free spirit. He parodies Maria's use of the word "exception." His repetition of the word "confine" with a new meaning is an instance of the figurative device called "ploce." Maria uses it in the sense of "keep," while Sir Toby switches to the sense of "dress." There's a sly defiance in this switch of senses that reflects his high-spirited nature. This example of "ploce" and others in this scene lend a sharp emphasis to the dialogue.

The scene ends with Sir Toby introducing a succession of "dance" images. This imagery both characterizes Sir Toby as the representative of partying that he is, and it strengthens the overall presence of a festival in Illyria.

Study Questions

1. Do we meet Olivia in this scene?
2. What is Sir Andrew's relationship to Sir Toby?
3. What did Maria hear about Sir Andrew's purpose for being in the house?
4. What does the presence of Maria and Sir Toby as characters imply?
5. Who brings in a note of competition to the scene?
6. Does Sir Andrew seem an appropriate suitor for Olivia?
7. What else do Sir Toby and Sir Andrew illustrate in the play?
8. How does Shakespeare reveal Sir Toby's free spirit?
9. What is "ploce"?
10. What type of imagery does Sir Toby introduce at the end of the scene?

Answers

1. No, we do not meet Olivia in this scene.
2. They are friends.
3. Maria heard that Sir Toby brought him to the house to woo Olivia.
4. They imply that love is for all kinds of people, no matter what their status is.
5. Sir Andrew brings in a note of competition.
6. No, the scene leaves us with the impression that Sir Andrew may not be an appropriate suitor for Olivia.
7. Sir Toby and Sir Andrew illustrate the party-and-fun atmosphere, as implied in the title's holiday.

8. Shakespeare reveals Sir Toby's free spirit through the language.

9. "Ploce" is the repetition of a word in a different sense.

10. Sir Toby introduces a succession of "dance" images.

Suggested Essay Topics

1. Sir Andrew may not be a good suitor for Olivia. Defend this thesis statement referring to specific examples from the dialogue.

2. Analyze the dance imagery found in lines 116–138. Why do you think Shakespeare included it in the dialogue? With what aspect of the play does it tie in? What does it emphasize?

Act I, Scene 4

Summary

We find Viola (now named "Cesario") on her fourth day in the Duke's palace, her disguise having gained her the access she wished. Valentine is amazed, in fact, at how much favor she has already gained with the Duke.

The Duke assigns Cesario the task of pursuing Olivia for him. He urges him to be aggressive: "Be clamorous and leap all civil bounds." The Duke is confident that Cesario can effectively persuade Olivia to respond to his true passion. Cesario is doubtful.

Part of the Duke's confidence owes to his intuition of Cesario's real feminine qualities. He implies, in other words, that she can play the womanly matchmaker role well. He promises him a reward if he is successful in his undertaking.

Viola's last lines allude to another plot strand in the play, her love for the Duke, which she cannot reveal because of her disguise.

Analysis

It is appropriate to consider a definition of the type of play (or "genre") that *Twelfth Night* is. *Twelfth Night* belongs to a species of drama known as "comedy." We expect the course of action in a comedy to be different from that in a tragedy. As M.H. Abrams puts it in *A Glossary of Literary Terms*:

> Romantic comedy, as developed by Shakespeare and some of his Elizabethan contemporaries, is concerned with a love affair that involves a beautiful and idealized heroine (sometimes disguised as a man); the course of this love does not run smooth, but overcomes all difficulties to end in a happy union.

Twelfth Night contains both of these elements and a lot more. The definition enlightens us about the ending; it will be a happy one. In comedy, love conquers all. Northrop Frye makes it clear that comedy is "community-oriented, its vision has a social significance. This vision calls for the establishing of society as we would like it." (Frye, 286)

Recall, therefore, that up until the fourth scene, the Duke's love is virtually the "talk of the town." Not only does the Duke brim with lyrical expression of his love, but the other characters are also aware of his infatuation. This tight interweaving of the Orsino courtship strand develops the love theme quite nicely.

This scene offers an inkling as to a slight alteration in the Duke's impassioned stance toward Olivia. Cesario's brief stay has exerted a subtle influence on him. Orsino closes the scene with a display of common sense that moves him momentarily away from the love-filled garden he's been in. He judges Cesario's ability to perform the errand and offers him wealth if he succeeds.

Study Questions

1. What is Viola's male name?

2. What task does the Duke assign Cesario?

3. For whom does Cesario feel love for?

4. To what genre does the play *Twelfth Night* belong?

5. What kind of an ending do we expect in comedy?

6. What kind of vision does comedy have, according to Northrop Frye?

7. What is the community of Illyria doing about the Duke's love?

8. How does the Duke respond to Cesario's doubts that Olivia is too "abandoned to her sorrow" to listen to his suit?

9. Does the Duke change?

10. What does Orsino display at the end of the scene?

Answers

1. Viola's male name is "Cesario."

2. The Duke assigns Cesario the task of pursuing Olivia for him.

3. Cesario feels love for the Duke.

4. *Twelfth Night* belongs to the genre of "comedy."

5. We expect a happy ending in comedy.

6. Comedy's vision has a social significance.

7. The community in Illyria is well aware of and talking about the Duke's love.

8. The Duke tells him to "be clamorous and leap all civil bounds."

9. The Duke's impassioned stance toward Olivia changes slightly.

10. Orsino displays common sense at the end of the scene.

Suggested Essay Topics

1. Think of your efforts to win a sweetheart when you've fallen in love, or what you might do to win one. In what ways would those efforts be similar or different from Cesario's endeavors to woo Olivia for the Duke?

2. Consider once again the definition of "Romantic comedy" stated earlier. Why do you think the society of a given era would desire a happy ending? Would you like to see *Twelfth Night* end in another way than it does?

Act I, Scene 5

New Characters:

Olivia: *the countess with whom Orsino is in love and who rejects him*

Clown: *servant to Olivia who sings and provides entertainment*

Malvolio: *steward to Olivia*

Summary

This scene opens with Maria and the Clown engaged in conversation. Maria, wondering where the Clown has been, tells him that he'll be punished for his absence unless he has good reason for it. This threat fails to scare the Clown, as he shows in his offhand replies.

The Clown is equally offhand with Olivia when she enters. He responds to her with insult, ironically calling her a "fool." Although she tries to get rid of him, the Clown prevails on her to prove that she is the fool. To that end, he questions her about her mourning her brother's death.

Unoffended, Olivia turns to her steward Malvolio for his opinion of the Clown. An exchange of insults follows her question. The Clown puts down Malvolio and Malvolio puts down the Clown. Malvolio considers the Clown a stupid, useless character. Olivia sides with the Clown, even calling Malvolio an "egotist," because the Clown is only playing his role as "fool" properly.

Maria announces Cesario's arrival. Olivia is not in the mood to listen to a suit from the Duke. Malvolio returns to Olivia to tell her that Cesario stubbornly refuses to leave until Olivia will speak with him. Olivia wonders what kind of man he is. She allows him to enter and puts on a veil.

Cesario begins by showering lover's compliments on Olivia. Cesario makes a point of the fact that her suit is memorized. Everything he will say has been rehearsed beforehand.

Shortly after starting his speech of love, Cesario requests to see Olivia's face. Olivia complies and is met with praise for her "beauty truly blent." Cesario further affirms the Duke's passion for Olivia, expressing a hope that Olivia will reciprocate the Duke's love.

Unfortunately for the Duke, Olivia has no desire to love him. Cesario does not quite believe her rejection of Orsino. He can do little more than express a hope that Olivia will return the Duke's love, before he exits.

Olivia then reveals that she has been taken with the youth. His charms have worked their subtle ways on Olivia's eyes. So, she sends Malvolio after him with a token of her newfound affection, a ring. Her final words intimate some confusion about what is happening to her.

Analysis

The original love connection of the Duke admiring Olivia has gone awry by the end of this scene. We witness two twists: Viola states her attraction to Orsino, and Olivia reveals a liking for Cesario. These two twists suggest that, for Shakespeare, love is truly a subjective experience. When a person sees a potential sweetheart and falls in love, he or she feels it in his or her own heart and mind. One cannot be forced to love another by the sheer strength of the other's attraction, as the Duke's suit might imply.

Another way that Shakespeare emphasizes the subjective nature of love is through the Clown's speech. The Clown stands in counterpoint to the Duke in respect to his attitude toward Olivia. The smitten Duke utters his passionate feeling for Olivia, but the Clown's insults are couched in a jarringly logical manner. The former exalts Olivia; the latter belittles her. The Clown insists on proving Olivia a "fool." This slighting of Olivia reveals her to be a real person rather than the idealized goddess that the Duke opens the play with.

Shakespeare's plays have fools and clowns in them, whose speech very often has relevance to the action. The most famous example is Lear's fool, who utters profound commentary on Lear's plight. The Clown's role in *Twelfth Night* is a bit more subtle. As noted, the Clown's self-conscious reference to words and logic provide an indirect commentary on the Duke's love.

In an obvious way, the Clown is the clown of the party in the play. His wordplay and attitude toward Olivia demonstrate that he's enjoying the amusement that is found in a festive atmosphere. In keeping with the fun-filled atmosphere, Sir Toby makes a drunken entrance to comment briefly on Cesario's arrival.

Cesario's prepared speech for Olivia, on Orsino's behalf, contains an extended theological metaphor, which Olivia picks up on and carries forward. Cesario contends that he has a sacred message for Olivia. The loftiness of the theological metaphor reflects the great value placed on Orsino's suit. His love is sacred; Olivia is his goddess. A special bond is thus formed between Cesario and Olivia in view of the way Olivia responds to the theological language of his speech. Perhaps she is valuing the speaker more than the speech.

Cesario finishes his effort to persuade Olivia with speech that has not been studied. He includes hyperbole to emphasize the Duke's passion. (1. 256) Cesario earnestly believes that Olivia should return the Duke's offer of love. He regards her closed-mindedness as cruel.

Study Questions

1. What does Maria threaten the Clown with?
2. What kind of attitude does the Clown evidence toward Olivia?
3. What does the Clown try to prove about Olivia?
4. What is the name of Olivia's steward?
5. What does Olivia put on before speaking with Cesario?
6. Who falls in love with whom in this scene?
7. What do the two love twists we've witnessed suggest?
8. Which character serves to emphasize the subjective nature of "love" ?
9. In what manner are the Clown's insults couched?
10. What type of metaphor does Cesario use to lend emphasis to the great love the Duke holds for Olivia?

Answers

1. Maria threatens the Clown with punishment for his absence.
2. The Clown evidences an offhand attitude toward Olivia.

3. The Clown tries to prove that Olivia is a fool.

4. Malvolio is Olivia's steward.

5. Olivia puts on a veil before speaking with Cesario.

6. Olivia falls in love with Cesario.

7. The love twists suggest just how subjective is the experience of love.

8. The Clown's speech emphasizes the subjective nature of "love."

9. The Clown's insults are couched in a jarringly logical manner.

10. Cesario uses an extended theological metaphor to reflect the Duke's great love.

Suggested Essay Topics

1. How does the Clown prove that Olivia is a fool? Is he correct or incorrect in his assessment? Explain your answer with evidence found in the text.

2. How many love strands does the first act contain? Who is involved in them? Where do the relationships stand by the end of Act I in relation to how they will eventually develop?

Act II

Act II, Scene 1

New Characters:

Antonio: *a sea captain, friend to Sebastian, who wishes to serve him*

Sebastian: *Viola's twin brother, who survives the shipwreck and initially believes Viola has drowned*

Summary

This short scene serves the purpose of letting us know that Sebastian, Viola's twin brother, has reached the shores of Illyria. We need this information to prepare our understanding of later scenes.

Sebastian tells us a little about himself, thus informing us that he has a twin sister. He thinks that she drowned while he managed to gain safety.

He wishes to separate from Antonio and wander about the area. But shortly afterward, he contradicts himself in this intention by stating that he, specifically, wants to go to "the Count Orsino's court." Although Antonio offers to serve Sebastian, he cannot go immediately with him to Orsino's court because he has "many enemies" there. Yet, we will learn that Antonio's affection for Sebastian is strong enough to prompt him to follow after him eventually.

Analysis

Notice the very straightforward and formal manner in which these men talk to one another. Since this scene serves an informative purpose, the formal dialogue is most appropriate. There is very little poetry in this scene. They are not expressing their love for a woman as Orsino was doing in the first scene. The dialogue serves up numerous indications that its purpose here is just to inform. Antonio starts the dialogue with a straightforward yes-or-no question: "Will you stay no longer?" Sebastian gives his answer. Then Antonio makes a request whose very words explicitly suggest that this scene is providing the audience with information: "Let me know of you whither you are bound." Finally, Sebastian states background information in his next speech.

The contrast between the formal prose of this scene and the poetry of the love speeches should teach us about Shakespeare's use of language. Poetry expresses feeling, often strong feeling, so using it to reveal the depth of one's love is a fine touch. Prose aims to inform and enlighten us about a particular subject or issue, and it is often, though not always, free of the embellishments and imagination of poetry.

The use of shipwrecked twins in a romantic plot, such as in *Twelfth Night,* is not an idea original to Shakespeare. As with most of his plays, he used source materials to inspire him with characters and plots. L.G. Salingar enlightens us as to the way in which Shakespeare manipulated his sources:

> There are four essential characters to Gl'Ingannati [a Sienese comedy], Bandello [story], Riche [story], and Shakespeare; namely, a lover, a heroine in his service disguised as a page, her twin brother (who at first has disappeared), and a second heroine. The basic elements common to all four plots are: the heroine's secret love for her master; her employment as go-between, leading to the complication of a cross-wooing; and a final solution by means of the unforeseen arrival of the missing twin.

Even Shakespeare's mastery required original source materials on which to work.

Study Questions

1. What is Antonio's occupation?

2. What relation does Sebastian hold to Viola?

3. What does Sebastian think has happened to Viola?

4. Where do Antonio and Sebastian find themselves in this scene?

5. What purpose does this scene serve?

6. How would you characterize the style of the dialogue?

7. Where does Sebastian say he is headed?

8. What does Antonio want to do for Sebastian?

9. Name one source for *Twelfth Night*.

10. Essentially, what do the sources and the play *Twelfth Night* have in common?

Answers

1. Antonio is a sea captain.

2. Sebastian is Viola's brother.

3. Sebastian thinks that Viola has drowned.

4. They find themselves on Illyria's shore.

5. The purpose of this scene is to inform us about Viola's twin brother.

6. The style is one of formal, straightforward prose.

7. Sebastian says he is headed for Orsino's court.

8. Antonio wishes to serve Sebastian.

9. The sources for *Twelfth Night* are Gl'Ingannati, Bandello, and Riche.

10. The sources have the four essential characters and the plot in common with Shakespeare.

Suggested Essay Topics

1. Name one characteristic of poetic language and one of prose. After you state those, select one speech in the play that contains poetry and another from Act II, Scene i that contains prose, and explain the differences you notice between the two. Allow your imagination to explore the significance of the two different styles.

2. An important issue to be aware of when discussing characters' motivations and fates is that of "free will" versus "determinism or fate." Define these two concepts. And then, consider lines 3–8, spoken by Sebastian, in the light of that issue. Does Sebastian feel that he is in full control of things?

Act II, Scene 2

Summary

Malvolio catches up with Cesario to give him the ring from Olivia. Naturally, he is surprised inasmuch as he knows he did not leave a ring. Malvolio also repeats Olivia's desire not to have any further dealings with Orsino. Before leaving, Malvolio puts the ring on the ground.

Left alone on stage, Cesario utters a soliloquy in which he expresses his confusion over the ring. He now realizes that Olivia has fallen in love with him. "She loves me sure," he asserts. He acknowledges that the disguise must be responsible for stirring up her love. He finishes up the soliloquy wondering how this mistaken love on his part and frustrated love on his master's part will be resolved. As matters currently stand, there is a mess for all the lovers involved. Time will bring in the solutions.

Analysis

It is useful to understand the function of a soliloquy in drama. Sometimes a playwright cannot include important information about character or plot in the dialogue, so a soliloquy may become necessary.

> Soliloquy is the act of talking to oneself, silently or aloud. In drama it denotes the convention by which a character, alone on the stage, utters his thoughts aloud; the playwright uses this device as a convenient way to convey directly to the audience information about a character's motives, intentions, and state of mind, as well as for purposes of general exposition. (Abrams, 180)

In this scene, Cesario certainly makes an important commentary about the love situation while alone on stage. A soliloquy like the one he utters is true to the character of Cesario we've seen so far.

His words continue to reflect his role as representative of the practical, commonsense aspect of love in this play. He very logically takes account of Olivia and Orsino's feelings. True, he may be capable of such intense feelings for another person, but he realizes that people have to get along in the real world each day, too. This play gives us the feeling that the depiction of love would somehow be incomplete if it emphasized just the romance and passion of Orsino and Olivia's feelings. Love can still see the beloved as an ordinary human being.

Critics have argued over how to interpret Malvolio. The issue relates to Malvolio's character and the significance of the comic plot centered on him. Consider how dutiful and nonchalant he appears in this scene. He brings the ring, delivers Olivia's message, and takes off. We can start to form our opinion of his character.

In his soliloquy, Cesario repeats the motif of "appearances versus reality." Every instance of a motif should enhance our understanding of the playwright's views on that particular subject.

> Disguise, I see thou art a wickedness
> Wherein the pregnant enemy does much.
> How easy is it for the proper false
> In women's waxen hearts to set their forms!

These lines express his concern that appearances are deceiving. In this context, Olivia has fallen in love with Cesario's outer masculinity, which causes him to realize that a mask can lead someone into love, regardless of the true character of the person beneath it. It is not Cesario's intention, however, to seduce Olivia.

Study Questions

1. Why does Malvolio seek Cesario?

2. Whose ring is it?

3. What kind of speech is it that Cesario utters?

4. What does Malvolio emphasize to Cesario?

5. Where does Malvolio put the ring?

6. What does Cesario feel about the ring?

7. Who has fallen in love with Cesario?

8. What does Cesario wonder in the latter part of the soliloquy?

9. What motif does Cesario repeat in his soliloquy?

10. What is the critics' attitude toward Malvolio?

Answers

1. Malvolio seeks Cesario to give him a ring.

2. It is a ring from Olivia.

3. Cesario utters a soliloquy.

4. Malvolio emphasizes that Olivia wants Orsino to stop his wooing.

5. Malvolio places the ring on the ground.

6. Cesario feels confused about the ring.

7. Olivia has fallen in love with Cesario.

8. Cesario wonders how the mistaken love will be resolved.

9. Cesario repeats the motif of "appearances versus reality."

10. Critics have argued over how to interpret Malvolio.

Suggested Essay Topics

1. Does Cesario's soliloquy add to our knowledge of character or plot? Read lines 17–41 carefully and explain your answer. Be sure to specify whose character and which plot.

2. Look carefully at the couplet closing Cesario's soliloquy: "O Time, thou must untangle this, not I;/It is too hard a knot for me t'untie." To what knot is he referring? How does this knot eventually become unravelled in the play? How is this resolution instructive in respect to the theme of love?

Act II, Scene 3

Summary

In case we'd forgotten about the merriment of the play, this scene puts us back in Olivia's house and opens with the leader of the party, Sir Toby. If we follow the love plot of the previous scene, we are then led astray by what these two men say. They begin by talking about going to bed early. Sir Toby says that going to bed after midnight is equal to going to bed early. Toby calls for some wine to have with their food.

When Feste the Clown enters, Andrew compliments his singing voice and his skill displayed in entertainment the previous night: "Why, this is best fooling, when all is done." Then, continuing in this vein, Sir Toby calls for another frequently used element in Shakespeare's plays—a song. Feste suggests either a love song or a song with a moral. Naturally, a love song is apropos. The Clown sings a song that recalls the Duke's elevated emotion of the first scene; he also defines "love." Very pleased with the Clown's song, they engage him in some more singing.

Nevertheless, Maria enters and chides them for their nonsense. Sir Toby banters with her, as is appropriate to his role as "lord of misrule," (to use the holiday expression). Malvolio's questions refer to their purpose as the merrymakers in the play. His question, "Do ye make an alehouse of my lady's house?", best points up the intersection of the holiday atmosphere and the love theme, which constitutes the play's peculiar blend. Malvolio seriously restates his lady's displeasure with Sir Toby's revels. What follows, to Malvolio's chagrin, is more singing and wine-drinking. Malvolio departs with an insult from Maria.

It is at this point that the comic plot is hatched. Maria reveals that she wants revenge on Malvolio, and Sir Toby and Andrew go

right along with her scheme. Maria believes that she is wreaking revenge on Malvolio's Puritan character. Maria explains the plot: it involves dropping letters in Malvolio's way, supposedly written by Olivia (in her own hand), which will lead him to believe that Olivia is professing her love to him. They are to delight in the spectacle.

Analysis

This scene is a good illustration of what L.G. Salingar (quoting Enid Welsford) characterizes as Shakespeare's transmuting "into poetry the quintessence of the Saturnalia." There is plenty of wine and singing running through a scene that also gives us the springboard for Malvolio's pending humiliation. To clarify this important element of the play, Salingar further adds, "The sub-plot shows a prolonged season of misrule, or 'uncivil rule,' in Olivia's household, with Sir Toby turning night into day; there are drinking, dancing, and singing,…and the gulling of an unpopular member of the household." So, by this point, the significance of the title should be quite clear.

It is noteworthy how appropriate the song from Feste the Clown is, for it defines love. This is a play that illustrates the theme of love, showing a particular vision of the love experience. The song is divided into two halves: the first half resembles the outpourings that we've already read from the Duke. It expresses praise and longing for the love object. The second half embodies the theme, "What is love?" The definition emphasizes the intensity of feeling such as the Duke has shown. Thus it has little relevance to Cesario's role in the play. There is a double-faceted nature to love. (Some may even see or feel more facets.) Willard Gaylin puts it this way in his *Rediscovering Love*:

> Obviously loving and being loved can and should coexist in one relationship—there is no real conflict between the two. One may so dominate the psychological needs of an individual as to exclude the other [as we clearly see with Orsino], but they have a natural compatibility. (Gaylin, 108)

In the opening scene, the Duke has no relationship with Olivia as he utters his love. Cesario enters his service to engender a loving relationship for him.

As for the controversy surrounding Malvolio, there is no reason to expect that he take part in the revelling. So, Maria's criticism of his being too straitlaced doesn't hold a lot of water. He performs his service earnestly and dutifully for his lady. We ought to ponder whether revenge is a fitting motive for the deception to follow. Some readers might conclude that Maria and Sir Toby resent Malvolio because he appears moralistic and judgmental.

Study Questions

1. What does going to bed after midnight mean for Sir Toby?

2. What does Sir Andrew call Feste the Clown?

3. What ability of the Clown does Sir Andrew compliment?

4. What do Sir Toby and Andrew offer to Feste for his singing?

5. What two types of songs does the Clown suggest?

6. What does the Clown's song define?

7. In keeping with the holiday tradition, what title can we apply to Sir Toby?

8. What plot is hatched in this scene?

9. What is Maria's motive for the scheme?

10. What does Maria plan to drop in Malvolio's way?

Answers

1. For Sir Toby, going to bed after midnight means going to bed early.

2. Sir Andrew calls Feste "the fool."

3. Sir Andrew compliments the Clown's singing voice.

4. They offer him money.

5. The Clown suggests either a love song or a song with a moral.

6. The Clown's song defines "love."

7. Sir Toby can take on the title of the "lord of misrule."

8. The comic plot is hatched in this scene.

9. Maria's motive for the scheme is revenge.

10. Maria plans to drop letters in Malvolio's way.

Suggested Essay Topics

1. Describe the fun and festive atmosphere that makes up most of this scene. What role does Feste the Clown play in it? Cite specific lines to strengthen your description. Do you enjoy the playfulness? Why or why not?

2. Analyze Maria's speeches in this scene. Explain carefully her motive to entrap Malvolio. Do you believe that she is justified in doing it?

Act II, Scene 4

Summary

In this scene, we are back at the Duke's palace. Once again, the Duke wants to hear some music, the food for his love. He calls for the Clown, who happens not to be there at the moment. While waiting for the Clown to be located, he speaks with Cesario.

The Duke affirms his true love. He continues to be the passionate lover who yearns for his beloved. His emotions, as a lover, are topsy-turvy.

The Duke surmises that Cesario had once also been in love, as he currently is. He answers "yes" that she was of the same age and temperament as the Duke. He responds with his belief that the woman should be the younger of the pair, so as to ensure that the love remain robust.

The Clown returns and Orsino is eager for a love song, a song that deals with the innocence of love, such as he is experiencing. The emphasis in the Clown's song is prophetic. It focuses on the Duke's frustration with and failure to obtain Olivia, his heart's desire. The lover in the song is "slain by a fair cruel maid." In short, it's a song of unrequited love.

Interestingly, in spite of the Duke's praise for this song, the Clown insults Orsino in a manner similar to the way he insulted Olivia in Act I. The Clown suggests that he lacks consistency and

direction, though the logical form of his expression is not so apparent as in his insult to Olivia.

The Duke sends Cesario to Olivia to woo her for him. Cesario warns him that Olivia is not open to romance with him. Cesario asks the Duke if he would love a woman just because she had an intense attraction to him. The Duke does not think that that is a valid comparison, suggesting that a man's love is more powerful. Cesario disagrees with the Duke's proposition. Women are capable of very strong love attachments. Cesario, in fact, refers to his father's daughter as an example.

Analysis

The Duke wants to hear some music. This is the same request he makes at the start of Act I. This suggests that his love is still strong. The frustration has failed to extinguish the fire in his heart. Again, he is in the passive role of wanting the music to work on his feelings. His request for Feste to sing again should also remind us of the festive spirit.

As the Duke speaks to Cesario, we find him in the same infatuated frame of mind as in previous scenes. Shakespeare thus illustrates the love theme. The Duke is in the state of "loving" (in Gaylin's terms). He is not yet in the condition that Cesario perhaps represents.

Cesario presents more evidence that he is in touch with the reality of the situation. After the Duke requests that he go to Olivia to sue, Cesario counters with an eye-opening question: "But if she cannot love you, sir?" Not only does the Duke's answer suggest that his love continues intense, but it also demonstrates that love has a will of its own that may run at variance with reality. "No" is not a viable answer for him. In this way, Cesario is trying to reason with Orsino. Just because he is in love with Olivia, it doesn't follow that Olivia will fall in love with him.

The song Feste sings is prophetic, so it relates to the theme in a forward-looking manner. It expresses the death of love, which, in view of the Duke's confidence, may astonish the reader. The Duke feels that Olivia should reciprocate his love. But there's a song that tells of a "fair, cruel maid," who is obviously Olivia, who has killed her wooer. Cesario has already referred to Olivia as "fair cruelty."

Olivia never accepts the love of Orsino. To the passionate lover, such rejection is tantamount to murder. So intense are the rejected lover's feelings that he desires to be buried in a grave. This intensity is fitting for Orsino, who has already expressed such passionate feelings for his beloved.

Study Questions

1. What is the first item the Duke requests?
2. Who is not immediately available to sing the song?
3. What kind of a lover does Orsino classify himself as?
4. What does the Duke surmise about Cesario?
5. According to the Duke, does the age of the man in a relationship matter?
6. What does the Clown's song focus on?
7. Who does the Clown insult?
8. Where does Cesario go once again?
9. What warning does Cesario give to Orsino about Olivia?
10. In what does the lover of the Clown's song wish to be laid?

Answers

1. The Duke requests some music.
2. The Clown is not immediately available to sing the song.
3. Orsino classifies himself as a "true lover."
4. The Duke surmises that Cesario has been in love.
5. Yes, the age of the male partner does matter.
6. The Clown's song focuses on the Duke's frustration with and subsequent failure to obtain Olivia.
7. The Clown insults the Duke.
8. Cesario goes to woo for the Duke.
9. Cesario warns the Duke that Olivia is not open to romance with him.
10. The lover is ready to be buried in a coffin.

Suggested Essay Topics

1. Analyze the song in this scene. Who and what is involved in it? Which *Twelfth Night* character does it relate to? Explain your answer.

2. Why does the Duke believe that the man should be older than the woman in a relationship? Consider lines 29–39. Do you agree with his opinion? Why or why not?

Act II, Scene 5

New Character:

Fabian: *the servant to Olivia who is the third spectator to Malvolio's humiliation*

Summary

This scene is devoted exclusively to the devious comic plot. Sir Toby gathers Fabian, another servant, and Andrew to enjoy the exercise in shame that Maria is about to execute. Fabian seems to have a bone to pick with him, so he is interested in what will happen to Malvolio.

Maria has the whole trick worked out. They will hide in a box tree and observe as Malvolio picks up the falsified letter to read it. Olivia is on Malvolio's mind when he enters. Sir Toby and Fabian believe that Malvolio's arrogance makes him suitable game for the trap that's been set. Malvolio fancies himself a suitor to Olivia.

Speaking aloud, Malvolio continues to let his imagination run wild over the prospect of loving Olivia and the accompanying self-aggrandizement. While doing so, Sir Toby, Fabian, and Andrew devilishly comment on his behavior. That they are sadistic in intention is evident in such remarks as "Pistol him, pistol him" and "O for a stonebow, to hit him in the eye."

Eventually Malvolio sees the letter, which appears to him to be in Olivia's handwriting. Though it is a love letter, it doesn't completely mention Malvolio by name. Malvolio takes the declaration of love to be addressed to him because it identifies the beloved as

"M,O,A,I," four letters that can be found in Malvolio's name. Furthermore, the phrase "I may command where I adore" leads him to believe that he is the man because he is her servant.

The letter goes on to suggest that fortune is now smiling on Malvolio. The letter also induces him to adopt peculiar behaviors. He is to be hostile with a kinsman, smile in Olivia's presence, study political treatises for advice, and wear yellow stockings and cross-garters. Malvolio, convinced of the letter's authenticity, resolves to follow all of its suggestions.

Sir Toby foreshadows his subsequent marriage to Maria in this scene. He is so intrigued by her skill in the trap that he cannot help feeling love for her: "I could marry this wench for this device."

As yet, Malvolio has not humiliated himself before Olivia. The scheme will come to fruition when Malvolio confronts Olivia with smiles and yellow stockings, cross-gartered. So, for this devilish group, the best is yet to come.

Analysis

"Whether Malvolio has been most notoriously abused, or whether he is the well-deserving victim of a practical joke that explodes his vanity, social-climbing, and pretentiousness is the point at issue," says Maurice Charney. Until the device of Maria's letter, the play does not firmly emphasize Malvolio's vanity and social-climbing. As has been shown, he properly carries out his duty for Olivia. Only through what other characters say of him may we feel justified in labeling him an "overweening rogue," as Sir Toby does. His behavior, though, is quite proper.

What we should come to terms with is the relationship of this comic plot to the other plot. What it has in common, of course, is the theme of love. Malvolio is duped into believing that Olivia loves him, and he falls in love. This "symbolist drama," as Ralph Berry terms it, becomes a perversion of Orsino's love for Olivia. Malvolio may be likened to the Duke in the way that the letter ignites his passion for her. The letter, as a practical means of expression, reminds us of Cesario's position in the total rendering of the love theme. But, since the letter is a trick, Malvolio's love is a parody of the feelings and behavior of the Duke and Cesario. Olivia does not, nor will she, love Malvolio.

Perhaps the most glaring instance of perverseness is in the endings of the plots. Comedy prescribes a happy ending for the lovers in the romantic plot. Maria's contrived plot only issues forth a cruel outcome for Malvolio. The letter contains no truth. Malvolio will go mad.

This scheme is too cruel to be characterized as a bit of sport in keeping with the festive atmosphere. The desire for revenge that Sir Toby and Maria reveal undermines the acceptability of such as "jest," as Sir Toby euphemistically calls it. Malvolio is alienated from the rest of the household, and the way in which its members so handily trap him, "the woodcock near the gin," emphasizes his alienation. From the moment Malvolio enters, he is unaware of the others in the box tree. His lines are interspersed with the reactions of the spectators, with neither side being able to hear the other. This gives us a physical representation of the psychological phenomenon of "alienation." The spectators enjoy the device on Malvolio at the expense of his pride and feelings.

It is evident why this plot element in the play has been puzzling to critics.

The spectators to the trick associate animal imagery with Malvolio throughout this scene. This imagery lays emphasis on both his alienation from them as human beings and their view of him as an egotistical fool. Sir Toby's first question to Fabian refers to Malvolio as a "sheep-biter," that is, sneaky dog. To Maria, he is the "trout that must be caught with tickling." For Fabian, he is alternately a "rare turkey cock" and a "woodcock near the gin." Sir Toby also uses a bird image after Malvolio has begun reading the letter. As these characters delight in the cruel scheme, they feel that they have Malvolio right where they want him. Reducing Malvolio in their eyes to animal status sharply conveys that feeling. Animals lack reason, so they are wrapped up in their own little worlds to the extent that they operate by instincts. Sir Toby, Fabian, Andrew, and Maria are presumably drawing a parallel between the animals' instinctual selfishness and Malvolio's egoism.

Study Questions

1. Who is Fabian?

2. What is his motive for tricking Malvolio?

3. Who has worked out the scheme?

4. Where will the spectators of the device hide?

5. What does Malvolio fancy himself?

6. What kind of intention do Sir Toby and Andrew evidence by their remarks?

7. In whose handwriting supposedly is the letter that Malvolio finds?

8. What four letters in the letter lead Malvolio to believe it is addressed to him?

9. What is the source of imagery used by Sir Toby, Andrew, Maria, and Fabian to characterize Malvolio's situation?

10. From whom is Malvolio alienated?

Answers

1. Fabian is another of Olivia's servants.

2. Fabian apparently has a bone to pick with Malvolio.

3. Maria has worked out the scheme.

4. The spectators will hide in a box tree.

5. Malvolio fancies himself a suitor to Olivia.

6. Sir Toby and Andrew evidence a sadistic intention.

7. The letter is supposedly in Olivia's handwriting.

8. "M,O,A,I" lead Malvolio to believe it is addressed to him.

9. They use animal imagery to enlighten us about Malvolio's situation.

10. Malvolio is alienated from the rest of the household.

Suggested Essay Topics

1. Make the argument that Sir Toby, Andrew, Maria, and Fabian are behaving cruelly toward Malvolio. Is their cruelty justified in the light of the whole play? Do you personally accept the gulling of Malvolio?

2. Write an essay on "the love letter." First of all, define what
   you think it is. Does Maria's dropped letter fit your definition? What do you think of the requests made in the letter?
   How would you compose your own real love letter.

Act III

Act III, Scene 1

Summary

Cesario and Feste the Clown are conversing in Olivia's garden. Cesario, of course, has arrived with the purpose of courting Olivia. Cesario begins by asking the Clown if he earns a living with his tabor. In addition to engaging Cesario in wordplay, the Clown comments on the arbitrariness of words. People can do whatever they like with them regardless of good or bad intentions. Cesario briefly turns the conversation to identifying the fool. Feste, as usual, cannot give her a straight answer. He answers ironically that Olivia has no fool until she marries the man who will accept the role. In a short span, the Clown mentions a beard for Cesario, coins earning interest, and the love story of *Troilus and Cressida*. The Clown then goes to fetch Olivia. While awaiting Olivia, Cesario praises Feste's skillfulness at being a fool.

Sir Toby and Andrew arrive before Olivia. Sir Toby informs Cesario that Olivia is eager to see him. Paradoxically, Cesario asserts that he is Olivia's servant as well as Orsino's because the Duke has put himself at Olivia's service. His servant therefore is also hers. Olivia insists that she does not want to hear anymore wooing. Orsino is out.

Olivia, recalling the ring, broaches the subject of love toward Cesario. Cesario, rather than accept her love, says that he feels pity for Olivia. Cesario faithfully suggests the Duke's love again only to

hear Olivia pour out her feelings of love for him: "I love thee so that, maugre all thy pride,/Nor wit nor reason can my passion hide." Cesario does not wish to form a relationship with Olivia or any woman.

Analysis

We are meant to note a kind of kinship between Feste and Cesario. Shakespeare establishes this kinship by means of the ploce in the opening dialogue. For example, when Cesario says that those who manipulate words can make them "wanton," meaning equivocal, Feste picks up on another sense of "wanton," that is, unchaste, in his response. They have used the same word but in different senses. To play on someone else's words shows an interconnection between the two characters' ways of thinking. Cesario appreciates the Clown and even pays him for acting his role as fool.

The Clown of this play is a wordsmith and logician, in addition to being a good singer of the thematic songs. It behooves us to question the Clown's self-conscious commentary about words and their logic. He even refers to himself as not the fool, but rather Olivia's "corrupter of words." In essence, the Clown indicates his understanding of the arbitrariness of words: "Words are grown so false I am loath to/prove reason with them." There is no necessary and sufficient relationship between words and the reality to which they refer. Therefore, people can so manipulate words to do and say what they want, whether or not the words are true to the reality of the situation. Keeping in mind Cesario's connection with the motif of "appearances versus reality," his appreciation for the Clown's sensitivity to that issue is readily understandable. This scene sketches the Clown/fool's role in the play. For the characters in the play, this role of fool has entertainment value, and for the readers, his words have relevance to the play's interpretation.

In his short soliloquy following the Clown's departure, Cesario reveals his appreciation for the skill Feste exercises: "And to do that well craves a kind of wit." If Cesario can appreciate this skill, he is certainly capable of exercising it himself. The Clown is attuned to the mood and quality of people with whom he practices his fooling. Although we can assert that the Clown is very talented in his use of words, the truth value of what he says about others is not so clear.

Cesario, who represents practical common sense for the lovers, is everywhere a most admirable character. He makes a diligent effort to woo on Orsino's behalf. Another way that Shakespeare demonstrates his good communication skills is in the way he uses the same metaphors as other characters. When Sir Toby uses a trade metaphor, "trade be to," to characterize Cesario's presence in the garden, Cesario responds with another expression drawn from the language of trade, "I am bound to your niece." Cesario understands and can get along with all the characters in the play.

Olivia discloses her love for Cesario in this scene. The fundamental irony is that Cesario is there on the Duke's behalf, but Olivia expresses love for Cesario. This creates a complication in the original plot. Not only has Olivia not reciprocated her love to Orsino, but she's also bestowed it on Cesario. At this point, although we should expect a happy resolution to this entanglement, the issue of who-joins-who is not clear in this scene. Olivia, in declaring her love, is in the state of "loving": Cesario does not accept her offer.

The one clue we have that Cesario cannot wind up with Olivia is the knowledge of his true gender. Cesario is really a woman, so he must be paired with a male. At this point, we can surmise that Cesario will form a relationship with Orsino, the man for whom his female self has already expressed an attraction. Herschel Baker argues that the delay in the happy ending derives from the characters' inability to know the truth about themselves. This brings in the issue of "self-knowledge." Not everyone knows who they are, what they believe, or what they really want out of life. Thus, Cesario's disguise represents any such intellectual and emotional confusion of the other characters in concrete terms. It is only when he unmasks at the end and the misconception is cleared up that they can feel a sense of liberation from their illusions. Self-knowledge is attained, according to this view. This view changes Cesario's place in the love theme.

Taking the plunge into the experience of love, as Orsino and Olivia amply demonstrate, appears easy enough. The important related step of cementing a bond between the two persons is not so easy. Understanding this truism makes Cesario an appealing and curious character in the play.

Study Questions

1. What instrument is the Clown holding?
2. Where does the Clown say he lives by?
3. Why is the Clown upset with words?
4. Rather than Lady Olivia's fool, what does Feste claim to be?
5. What does Cesario praise while waiting for Olivia?
6. Who declares love in this scene?
7. What is Olivia's response to Cesario's wooing for the Duke?
8. Between what two characters does Shakespeare establish a kinship?
9. What happens when wise men act foolishly?
10. According to Herschel Baker, what do the characters lack?

Answers

1. The Clown is holding a tabor.
2. The Clown says he lives by a church.
3. The Clown is upset with words because they are rascals whose bonds disgraced them.
4. Feste claims to be Olivia's "corrupter of words."
5. Cesario praises the Clown's skill as a fool.
6. Olivia declares her love for Cesario in this scene.
7. Olivia rejects the Duke.
8. Shakespeare establishes a kinship between Cesario and the Clown.
9. They betray their common sense.
10. The characters lack self-knowledge.

Suggested Essay Topics

1. Describe the way in which the Clown carries out his role as "fool." What functions does he see himself as performing?

Does he fulfill them as he thinks he should? Make a judgment at the end of your essay as to whether he is a necessary or superfluous character in the play.

2. As Olivia is in the process of revealing her feelings for Cesario, she makes use of metaphors drawn from the animal kingdom—lines 120–122 and lines 130–131. State what these animal metaphors are, and then explain their significance. How do they illuminate the depth of Olivia's feelings at the moment?

Act III, Scene 2

Summary

Sir Andrew is disappointed that Olivia has not shown an interest in him. He has seen her giving more attention to Cesario than to him. Fabian claims that Olivia was deliberately trying to exasperate Andrew so as to spur him to more aggressive action. Andrew should have seized the moment to prove his masculinity: "You should have banged the youth into dumbness." Having failed to act has put Andrew way out of Olivia's thoughts, unless he can act quickly to arouse her admiration with his valor. Andrew agrees.

Sir Toby's idea for Andrew to achieve Olivia's love is to challenge Cesario to a fight. A fight will kindle her admiration. Sir Toby tells Andrew to write out a provocative challenge—"Let there be gall enough in thy ink"—to Cesario. Despite this incitement, Sir Toby says he will not actually deliver the letter to the youth.

Sir Toby espies Maria with a term of affection. Maria informs them how hilarious Malvolio's deception has turned out. He has obeyed every point of the letter. She manifests her sadistic pleasure in the way he is so taken over by the letter.

Analysis

Sir Toby plays his role as "lord of misrule" in this scene as well as in others. No sooner has Sir Andrew conveyed his frustration at winning Olivia's hand than does Toby devise a hostile plan to get her attention. It might be more proper to designate someone to

court Olivia, as Cesario has done for Orsino, But, he instead tells Sir Andrew to write an inflammatory letter to Cesario, a letter Sir Toby does not intend to pass on. Sir Toby keeps the action lively, stirring up a fracas that has love as its dubious impetus.

Sir Toby's plan reveals, moreover, underlying masculine values. First of all, he proposes a fight, which is often considered a manly activity. Secondly, he and Fabian place a great value on "valor" as a stimulus to love. This statement of belief in valor as a "lovebroker" for Sir Andrew is more evidence of the breadth of the love theme. Love is very subjective. People may love another for varied reasons and in varying intensities. In Sir Toby's masculine world, the reputation of valor may lead a woman into love.

Maria comes in to report that her scheme is reaching its high point. She deems it odd that Malvolio has so naively accepted the contents of the letter to the point of following every item. She mentions the confrontation with Olivia that is about to take place. However perverse it may be, Malvolio's embarrassing descent into love is also indicative of the subjective nature of the experience of love. It's puzzling, however, why Malvolio was so ripe to fall for his lady—unless the reader accepts the argument that Malvolio is egotistical and arrogant.

Study Questions

1. What is Sir Andrew getting ready to do?

2. On whom does Andrew see Olivia bestow her affection?

3. What is Fabian's explanation for that favoritism?

4. What element does Fabian think will stir Olivia's passion?

5. What idea does Sir Toby come up with to help Sir Andrew?

6. What task does Sir Toby assign Sir Andrew?

7. What does Sir Toby not plan to do, though?

8. In what manner does Sir Toby hail Maria?

9. How does Maria describe Malvolio's absorption in the letter?

10. What role does Sir Toby continue to play well?

Answers

1. Sir Andrew is getting ready to leave.

2. Andrew sees Olivia bestow her affection on Cesario.

3. Fabian asserts that she is doing that to exasperate Andrew and to rouse him to some action.

4. Fabian thinks that valor will stir Olivia to passion.

5. Sir Toby comes up with the idea of a fight.

6. Sir Toby assigns a letter to Sir Andrew to be delivered to Cesario.

7. Sir Toby does not plan to deliver the letter.

8. Sir Toby hails Maria in an affectionate manner.

9. Maria describes Malvolio's absorption in the letter as hilarious.

10. Sir Toby continues to play the role of "lord of misrule" well.

Suggested Essay Topics

1. Articulate Fabian and Sir Toby's assumption about the strength of a man's valor in inciting love. Then write an opinion essay on whether you think valor, "machoness," manliness, etc. are all that are necessary to win a woman's love. Are they sound bases to build a love on? Explain your thesis.

2. Summarize briefly all the love connections up to this point. Even sound like a gossip. Tell who loves who and who has hopes of who. Then, in the remainder of the essay, explain who you think deserves to be together with whom. In other words, you be the matchmaker. (You don't have to agree with Shakespeare's resolution of the complications.)

Act III, Scene 3

Summary

This short scene lets us know that Sebastian and Antonio are making their way into the action; they have not been left out. Antonio explains to a grateful Sebastian that both love and concern for his safety urged him to catch up to the youth. Antonio knows the area; Sebastian does not.

Sebastian desires to do some sightseeing in town, to see the "memorials and the things of fame," but Antonio has to back out. Antonio is wanted by Orsino's court for his part in a previous incident at sea. Sebastian reckons that perhaps he has murdered. Not so; Antonio says he is only guilty of piracy.

Antonio gives his money to Sebastian in case he wishes to purchase something, while Antonio lays low. He also recommends an inn where they can meet (the Elephant). They agree to find each other there.

Analysis

This scene does advance the plot even though there is no mention of either character's being in love. Sebastian is Viola's twin brother. As far as the love theme is concerned, we can predict—since a theme should be coherently worked out—that just as Viola has a place in the love plot, so too will Sebastian. He is a missing link. Olivia, Orsino, and Cesario expressing love make an uneven number. One more is needed to make two couples. These two couples, as they will eventually turn out to be, constitute two of the three love knots that are realized by the end of the play. Malvolio's love comes to naught, however, and Sir Andrew never gets Olivia.

We have had plenty of exposure to Olivia, Orsino, and Cesario's brand of loving and being loved in the play. So, Shakespeare need not belabor the role that Cesario has represented as the practical, commonsense-oriented person in the relationship. It's the Cesarios that keep the relationship going from day to day. The family tie that exists between Viola and Sebastian also implies a thematic parallel between the two characters. Shakespeare's economy had no need to dramatize Sebastian's practicality.

Antonio is familiar with the Duke and his Illyria. He, unfortunately, has had a run-in with the Duke's men in the past, so he feels it necessary to hide his presence. Shakespeare keeps him involved in the plot in such a way that will call attention to the illusion created by Viola's disguise. Later on, Antonio will take Cesario for Sebastian.

Study Questions

1. What does Sebastian say he will not do to Antonio?
2. Where do they meet?
3. What encouraged Antonio to keep up with Sebastian?
4. How does Antonio describe the area they're in?
5. What does Sebastian desire to do in Illyria?
6. Why does Antonio have to decline Sebastian's offer to see the town?
7. What does Sebastian reckon Antonio has done?
8. What does Antonio say he is guilty of?
9. Who is the missing link in the love strands?
10. With what character does Sebastian have a similar thematic function?

Answers

1. Sebastian says he will not chide him.
2. They meet in a street.
3. Antonio's love and concern for Sebastian encouraged him to keep up.
4. Antonio describes the area as "rough and unhospitable."
5. Sebastian desires to go sightseeing.
6. Antonio has to decline Sebastian's offer to accompany him because he is a wanted man.
7. Sebastian reckons Antonio has murdered.

8. Antonio says he is guilty of piracy.

9. Antonio is the missing link in the love strands.

10. Sebastian and Viola have similar thematic functions.

Suggested Essay Topics

1. Why doesn't Antonio find love in this play? Is it because a play can only have so many major and minor characters? Does he deserve to be matched up with Olivia, Viola, or some other woman in Illyria?

2. How does Shakespeare render the relationship between Antonio and Sebastian? Compare their relationship to Sir Toby and Sir Andrew's. Discuss the importance of friendship in a play like *Twelfth Night*.

Act III, Scene 4

New Characters:

Servant: *the one who informs Olivia of Cesario's return*

First Officer: *one of the Duke's officials who comes to arrest Antonio*

Second Officer: *accompanies the First Officer to carry out the arrest*

Summary

Olivia, longing for Cesario and out of sorts, wonders where Malvolio is. Here, she commends his nature as agreeable to her. Maria alerts her to his agitated state: "He is sure possessed." In accordance with the letter, Malvolio is smiling about the place. Nonetheless, Olivia wants to see him because she feels as disturbed as he.

Malvolio speaks to Olivia as though she knew about the letter. His smiling doesn't fit the mood Olivia is in. After Malvolio refers to his cross-gartering, Olivia asks if there is something wrong. Malvolio only mentions the commands of the letter to explain his behavior. For the rest of the dialogue between them, Malvolio quotes directly from Maria's letter, while Olivia intersperses her bewildered replies. Having been subjected to this unaccountable behavior, Olivia considers Malvolio to be mad: "Why, this is very midsummer madness." At this point, a servant enters with news that Cesario has come.

In his soliloquy, Malvolio sounds convinced that Olivia is following the letter. So, her bewilderment was lost on him as he raved on. He thanks Jove for the divine assistance he's been given.

Sir Toby, along with Fabian and Maria, comes to investigate Malvolio's behavior. Malvolio assumes the hostility toward him that the letter commands, not listening to the mock sympathy Sir Toby demonstrates. Fabian and Maria's similarly mock sympathy must be false because they know he's still under the influence of the letter. When Malvolio leaves, the culprits reflect on Malvolio's absorption by the letter. Sir Toby foreshadows at Malvolio's madness and ordeal in the dark room.

Sir Andrew enters with his letter of challenge. Fabian compliments the phrasing of the letter, containing a challenge to a fight, as Sir Toby reads it aloud. Sir Andrew is then egged on to draw on Cesario in the orchard. Claiming that Sir Andrew's letter will not ring true for Cesario, Sir Toby chooses to convey the challenge by word of mouth in order to "drive the gentleman…into a most hideous opinion of his rage, skill, fury, and impetuosity."

Following this, there is a brief interlude involving Olivia and Cesario. Olivia complains that her protestations of love are falling on deaf ears. Part of her thinks that it is blameworthy to be so bold, but another part of her holds that love gives her the freedom to speak her love. Cesario likens Olivia's passion to Orsino's. Giving Cesario a jewel, Olivia asks him to return tomorrow. Olivia, conscious of her honor, wonders what it will inspire her to give Cesario. Cesario wants nothing but her return of love to the Duke. That is not possible for Olivia because she's given her love to Cesario. Olivia repeats her request for Cesario to come tomorrow.

When Olivia departs, Sir Toby alarms Cesario with the news that Sir Andrew is preparing to attack him. He urges Cesario to prepare to defend himself. Innocently Cesario cannot believe that he's done offense to anyone. Sir Toby counters that he has given cause for a fight. Sir Toby further tries to frighten Cesario with Sir

Andrew's strength and prowess. Sir Toby conjures an image of Sir Andrew as a valiant and well-connected knight who has three deaths in dueling to his credit. Cesario refuses to fight, it's not his way. So he seeks an escort from Lady Olivia.

Cesario surmises that Sir Andrew is only trying to test his valor. But Sir Toby explains that he has just cause. Cesario therefore must face the challenge. At Cesario's request, Sir Toby leaves to get Sir Andrew so he can tell him what offense Cesario has done. Fabian only admits to knowing that Sir Andrew is incensed against him. Fabian echoes Sir Toby's spurious praise of Sir Andrew's skill and power.

When Sir Toby finds Andrew, he scares him with an equally spurious account of Cesario's skill at fencing. Likewise, Andrew decides to avoid the duel, even offering his horse as a peace offering. Sir Toby supposedly rides off to make the proposal to Cesario. Cesario and Andrew are holding images of each other's hostility.

As these two men finally come together, Sir Toby alters the situation by claiming the cause not to be as grave as it was first thought to be. But, as a formality, they should have a duel. Sir Toby assures both of them that harm will not come of it.

After they draw, Antonio makes a timely entrance into the garden. His first impulse is to protect Cesario, who he believes is Sebastian. As soon as Sir Toby draws on Antonio, the Duke's officers enter. They recognize Antonio and arrest him. Antonio asks Cesario for some of the money he gave Sebastian. Cesario, though confused at this request (not being Sebastian), offers Antonio some of his own money. Antonio takes that as a denial and warns him that he will become angry at his ingratitude. Cesario affirms that Antonio is a stranger to him; Antonio cannot possibly hold a claim on him. Antonio recounts how he rescued Sebastian from drowning and showed him brotherly love. Antonio, feeling betrayed, leaves with the officers.

Cesario gathers that Antonio was referring to her brother, Sebastian. Realizing that he closely resembles his brother, Cesario fervently hopes that Antonio meant Sebastian.

Sir Toby judges Cesario a coward. This stirs up Sir Andrew's ire to fight, which is met with Sir Toby's command to give him a good thwacking.

Analysis

This is a lengthy scene in which Shakespeare draws together some of the loose ends of the love plot. Considering that Sebastian's presence is now signaled, this scene becomes the climax of the rising action. This revelation constitutes the major surprise, for the rest of the scene forms a logical continuation of plots that have been in motion since Act I. "This scene as a whole," according to L.G. Salingar, "with its rapid changes of mood and action, from Olivia to the subplot and back towards Sebastian, braces together the whole comic design."

In order for Malvolio's humiliation to be complete, he has to face Olivia under the influence of the letter. Olivia, at the start of the scene, has her mind on Cesario. She wants to see him and considers how she can best allure him. She speaks solemnly of Malvolio, "he is sad and civil," with whom she desires some fellowship. Maria alerts her to his mental agitation.

Malvolio's dialogue with Olivia is at once comic and perverse. We must laugh at the way he has been so duped by the other characters, as well as the way he carries the illusion until he is undeceived. The perversion of the love experience stands out prominently. Malvolio has the commands of the letter on his mind as he speaks to Olivia. Such love has no genuine source, as Orsino and Olivia's does. Malvolio elaborates on a love that Olivia has no idea of, nor has she any intention of falling in love with her servant. The only genuine element in this whole perverse matter is Malvolio's temporary infatuation. Shakespeare heightens the cruelty of the trick by having Maria play dumb and Olivia bespeak concern for his state of mind. Charles T. Prouty sums it up this way: "Thus the subplot may be seen as representing the obverse, the other side of the coin. In the main plot the characters move in the world of an established convention while in the other the characters are alien, if not antithetical, to the convention."

Sir Andrew returns to show Sir Toby the letter he has written. Sir Andrew has obviously taken a liking to Olivia; we have just not heard him utter his passion. Sir Toby's commonsense plan to interest Olivia in his friend partakes too much of the playful spirit of the play to qualify as reasonable interceding. Nonetheless, Sir Toby as the "lord of misrule" brings together these two major aspects of the play, love and foolery. Those two aspects intersect in the duel scene.

The interlude between Cesario and Olivia keeps their two distinct roles in the play sharply focused. The dialogue does not surprise us, so we can take pleasure in Cesario's consistency as representative of a practical quality. Olivia says that she has poured out her heart to a heart of stone. Cesario asserts his master's love, thus finely playing his role of intermediary.

In addition to blending the play's two key elements, the arranged fight between Cesario and Sir Andrew prepares the way for Antonio's timely rescue. Antonio comes upon the duel and believes he is saving his friend Sebastian. Regardless of whether the officers had come for him or not, it is evident that he would have made Sebastian's existence known. Upon his arrest, Antonio asks of Cesario the money he had given to Sebastian. The interchange that ensues finally brings out the name "Sebastian." Cesario's hope for her brother is revived.

Study Questions

1. How is Olivia feeling at the opening of the scene?

2. What does Olivia commend about Malvolio?

3. What influence sways Malvolio's mind as he speaks with Olivia?

4. In what words does Malvolio try to dismiss Sir Toby when he enters?

5. What does Sir Toby indicate his attitude toward Malvolio will be when the trick is done?

6. What does Sir Andrew return with?

7. How receptive is Cesario to Olivia's love?

8. With what news does Sir Toby alarm Cesario?

9. What does the knowledge of Sebastian's existence make of this scene?

10. How can we characterize Malvolio's dialogue with Olivia?

Answers

1. Olivia is out of sorts.

2. Olivia commends Malvolio's nature.

3. The commands of the letter sway Malvolio's mind as he speaks with Olivia.

4. Malvolio tries to dismiss Sir Toby with "Go off; I discard you."

5. Sir Toby indicates that he will show mercy on Malvolio when the trick is done.

6. Sir Andrew returns with the letter he wrote.

7. Cesario is not receptive to Olivia's love.

8. Sir Toby alarms Cesario with the report that Sir Andrew is preparing to attack him.

9. Knowledge of Sebastian's existence makes this a climactic scene.

10. We can characterize Malvolio's dialogue with Olivia as comic and perverse.

Suggested Essay Topics

1. Some critics have argued that Malvolio is presumptuous and arrogant. Discuss the extent to which those characteristics are responsible for his gulling and eventual madness. Support your case with evidence from the text.

2. Analyze this play in terms of its credibility and realism. To what extent is the action credible? To what extent is it fantasy and romance? Define the concepts you work with in your essay.

Act IV

Act IV, Scene 1

Summary

The Clown and Sebastian are talking in front of Olivia's house. Sebastian, unlike his sister, has not taken so well to Feste. They seem at odds with each other. Sebastian dismisses the Clown, maintaining that he has no business with him. The Clown, characteristically clever, responds by denying the reality of everything: "Nothing that is so is so." Indeed, Sebastian is not Cesario. Sebastian orders Feste to take his folly elsewhere. The Clown, clever though he be, is not omniscient, so he thinks that Sebastian is just pretending ignorance. He requests a message for Olivia. Sebastian dismisses him with an insult, but not without giving him a tip. The Clown is thankful.

Sir Andrew, Sir Toby, and Fabian enter. Sir Andrew immediately strikes Sebastian, mistaking him for Cesario. Though puzzled, Sebastian strikes multiple blows in return. Sir Toby joins the fray to help Sir Andrew by seizing Sebastian. After witnessing the fray, the Clown goes off to inform Olivia.

They continue the fight, with Sir Andrew threatening legal action and Sebastian ordering them to let go. Sebastian forcefully disentangles himself from their holds and warns them that on further provocation, he'll draw his sword. Apparently, Sir Toby cannot resist; he draws on Sebastian.

Olivia enters and surveys the scene to her distaste. The fracas

is yet another instance of Sir Toby's uncivilized tastes. She orders them to stop and get out. That her beloved (or the one she thinks is Cesario) is involved in the fight adds to her sense of offense. Olivia hopes that Sebastian will look rationally on the incident. She invites him to her house so she can tell him about Sir Toby's other "fruitless pranks."

Olivia's invitation baffles Sebastian. He wishes for further oblivion to add to the confusion he is experiencing. Yet, when Olivia repeats her invitation, he accepts.

Analysis

Critics disagree on how to interpret Feste's role. Despite Sebastian's attitude to Feste, the Clown and his role retain their dignity within the play. If anything, Sebastian depreciates the value of the Clown's content, that is, what it is he talks about. Cesario's praise for his wit, however, is well-taken. And his wit is clever in this scene. Although the Clown's songs have relevance to the theme and plot, the relevance of his dialogue is less clear. He is good with words and logic, and his displays of skill have proven quite entertaining, but whether he penetrates character and motive remains debatable. After all, in reality, Sebastian is not dissembling. Feste does not know he's with Sebastian instead of Cesario. L.G. Salingar puts it this way, "Feste is not the ringleader in *Twelfth Night*, nor is he exactly the play's philosopher." Similarly, Maurice Charney, in his chapter on *Twelfth Night*, discusses only Feste's agile mind at wordplay.

This is the scene in which Sebastian and Olivia are brought together, the foursome of the love plot is hence complete. Rightly so, the confusion seems all on Sebastian's part.

> What relish is in this? How runs the stream?
> Or I am mad, or else this is a dream.
> Let fancy still my sense in Lethe steep;
> If it be thus to dream, still let me sleep! (4.1.60–3)

This confusion arises out of the familiar way in which Olivia addresses Sebastian, whom she thinks is Cesario. Olivia has had dealings with Cesario already and expressed her love for him. In this scene, since they are twins, she thinks it is he. Sebastian does not fall in love with Olivia; rather, he puzzles over her familiarity. What does she mean, he wonders. The whole situation seems so unreal that he thinks he may have lost his senses. Yet he goes along with Olivia, perhaps taking pleasure in the illusion. He asks for oblivion so he can prolong the dream that Olivia is sustaining. To the extent that Sebastian's analogous role (to his sister's) is a necessary component to the love theme, his acquiescence in Olivia's dream is very likely. One of the complications of the plot is about to be cleared up, and the genre's happy ending is happily in the offing.

Study Questions

1. How does Sebastian react to Feste?
2. What does Sebastian tell the Clown to vent elsewhere?
3. Who tells the other to abandon his pretense?
4. Who fights in this scene?
5. When the Clown sees the fray, what does he do?
6. Who breaks up the fight?
7. How does Olivia characterize Sir Toby's behavior?
8. To whom does Olivia issue an invitation?
9. How does Sebastian respond to Olivia's invitation?
10. What does Maurice Charney say about Feste's mind?

Answers

1. Sebastian dismisses the Clown.
2. Sebastian tells the Clown to vent his folly elsewhere.
3. Feste tells Sebastian to abandon his pretense, "ungird thy strangeness."
4. Sebastian, Sir Andrew, and Sir Toby fight in this scene.
5. The Clown goes off to inform Olivia.
6. Olivia breaks up the fight.
7. Olivia calls Sir Toby a "rudesby" and "ungracious wretch."
8. Olivia issues an invitation to Sebastian.

9. Sebastian is surprised at Olivia's invitation.

10. Maurice Charney says that Feste has an "agile mind at word-play."

Suggested Essay Topics

1. In what way do Viola–Sebastian constitute a "poetic symbol," as one critic has said. In other words, if they are one spirit in two bodies, how does that technique help us to understand Shakespeare's vision of love in the play? Be careful to explain the symbolism before you construct your argument.

2. Discuss Olivia's attitude toward the brawl she comes upon. Find other places in the play where Sir Toby's foolery is criticized and list them. Why do you think characters express disapproval for the festive behavior? How would the play stand without Sir Toby's merriment?

Act IV, Scene 2

Summary

Maria gives the Clown a gown and beard, apparently wishing to prolong the sham with Malvolio. Feste readily accepts the offer to play Chaucer's Sir Topas. He has a stereotyped notion of a curate and a student, which he doesn't fit, though he does account himself an honest man and a good citizen. Sir Toby enters, greeting him as a parson, and pushes him on to Malvolio.

The Clown, dressed as Sir Topas, visits Malvolio in a very dark room. Malvolio immediately orders Sir Topas to go to Olivia without specifying the contents of his message. Malvolio perceives himself as a wronged man. He says that to Sir Topas and, in the same breath, he asserts his sanity. Sir Topas responds with assurance of his own mildness. Malvolio insists that the house is dark and that his abusers have laid him in the darkness. Sir Topas points out that there are sources of light coming into the room. Malvolio suggests that it's perhaps a figurative darkness surrounding him as well as maintaining his sanity once again. Sir Topas

does not admit to any darkness, insinuating instead that Malvolio is full of perplexity.

Malvolio asks for a test of his sanity, to which Sir Topas responds with a question about Pythagoras' doctrine. Malvolio answers aptly, but Sir Topas does not admit his sanity.

According to Maria, Malvolio is so blinded he cannot even see the Clown's disguise. The Clown goes once more, at Sir Toby's prompting, to talk with Malvolio. Sir Toby shows that his sadism in the matter has not subsided. The reason he must stop the trick is Olivia's disapproval of his antics.

The second conversation between Malvolio and Sir Topas follows in the same vein as the previous one. This time, Malvolio requests a pen, ink, and paper with which he can write to Olivia. The Clown (as Sir Topas) persists in the contention that Malvolio is mad, which Malvolio vigorously rejects. Moreover, Malvolio's counterclaim of abuse in this scene provides compelling evidence of the validity of his perceptions. He has indeed been played with.

During this conversation, the Clown speaks to Malvolio as both the Clown and Sir Topas. When Malvolio realizes this, he asks the Clown to get him some paper and light. He wants to send a message to Olivia. The Clown, though agreeing to help, still cannot resist implying that Malvolio is mad.

The Clown ends this scene with a song, whose significance is a bit obscure but does bear relevance to Malvolio's present predicament.

Analysis

The Clown puts on an act in this scene. He goes to Malvolio's room disguised as a Chaucerian curate, Sir Topas. This performance is commendable to the extent that the Clown is fulfilling his role as jester. It is truly his role to entertain the others. The talent the Clown exhibits is also impressive. It is not easy to do all that he does in this play.

Maria shows that she wants to antagonize Malvolio and continue the cruel deception. The Clown operates more out of the requirements of his role than a desire to further vex Malvolio. What he says to Malvolio helps to illuminate Malvolio's character and the effect of the trick on him. Malvolio is certain that he has been wronged. The confidence with which he asserts the abuse builds our sympathy for him. He appears the undeserving victim of a cruel hoax. A man who can perceive the wickedness of abuse would probably not be the kind to foist abuse on others. His perception therefore is valid.

The Clown insinuates that he is mad. Malvolio maintains his sanity. His perception of his sanity is reinforced by his desire to communicate with Olivia. He knows he has humiliated himself before her, and the reasonable thing to do is to make amends. The impulse to communicate is a sound one. Presumably he wants to apologize and to show her that he is in possession of his faculties.

The darkness surrounding Malvolio symbolizes his alienation from the other members of the household, which has reached a grotesque level. The darkness also suggests more. It may symbolize the cruelty and lack of understanding of the other characters. They are the ones who have abused him as he eloquently maintains. The Clown points out that there are sources of light in the room. They just aren't illuminating a man who has been swooped down on by malicious associates. The darkness may symbolize the closedmindedness of the Puritans. His incarceration may be the "lack of freedom" of the Puritanical philosophy.

The image of darkness coupled with allusions to the Devil offer compelling evidence of bad intentions on the other characters' parts and Malvolio's sound character. Sir Topas' second speech to Malvolio reflects this: "Out hyperbolical fiend! How vexest thou this/Man!" Sir Topas states explicitly that the forces impinging on Malvolio are malicious.

Study Questions

1. What two articles does Maria give the Clown?

2. Whom does she want Feste to play?

3. What label does Sir Topas greet Malvolio with?

4. What kind of room is Malvolio in?

5. What are the two sources of light in that room?

6. How does Malvolio perceive himself?

7. What items does Malvolio request from Sir Topas?

8. What kind of test does Malvolio ask for?

9. Why does Sir Toby feel compelled to put a stop to the trick?

10. What image in the scene suggests the cruelty of Maria and Sir Toby?

Answers

1. Maria gives the Clown a gown and a beard.

2. Maria wants Feste to play Sir Topas.

3. Sir Topas greets Malvolio as "Malvolio the lunatic."

4. Malvolio is in a very dark room.

5. The two sources of light in the room are bay windows and clerestories.

6. Malvolio perceives himself as a wronged man.

7. Malvolio requests a candle, pen, ink, and paper from Sir Topas.

8. Malvolio asks for a test of his sanity.

9. Sir Toby feels compelled to put a stop to the trick because Olivia disapproves of his nonsense.

10. The darkness image suggests the cruelty of Maria and Sir Toby.

Suggested Essay Topics

1. Why does the Clown insist that Malvolio is mad? Whom do you believe, Malvolio or Sir Topas/Clown? If Malvolio is not mad, in your opinion, what does the Clown's insistence suggest about his role in the play? If Malvolio is mad, explain why you don't accept his contentions.

2. Analyze the song with which the Clown closes the scene. Is the allusion to the Devil in harmony with the preceding allusions in the scene? How does the song pass judgment on Malvolio?

Act IV, Scene 3

Summary

This scene is set in the garden, a fitting locale for the culmination of a love match. Sebastian tries to come to terms with his good luck in his opening soliloquy. This love match is so quick that we have no inkling as to Sebastian's feelings about love as an experience and as they relate to Olivia.

He tells us that she gave him a pearl. He marvels at his newfound sweetheart and discounts that he is mad. He wishes for Antonio, who he couldn't locate at the Elephant, and for his esteemed advice. The improbability of his good fortune leads him to doubt the reality of what has happened. Unlike Cesario, however, he doesn't reject Olivia's gift of love. When the thought crosses his mind that Olivia may be mad, he dispels it immediately with the knowledge that Olivia is such a competent and fit manager of the affairs of her household. His good instincts conclude that there's some kind of deception attaching to Olivia's love.

Olivia wastes no time in proposing marriage. She has brought a priest to Sebastian to marry them. She invites Sebastian to the nearby chapel to participate in the ceremony. She promises him confidentiality until such time as he becomes ready to divulge the news of their wedlock. Sebastian accepts, pledging his everlasting faithfulness.

Analysis

In this scene, one of the love matches is fully realized. Olivia and Sebastian marry. This is a hasty move for Sebastian, who accepts, but not for Olivia. She has been in love with his twin (Cesario) throughout the play. So, she feels a sense of triumph in gaining her beloved. Sebastian, on the other hand, should express the surprise and wonder that he does. The play hitherto has given us little knowledge of his thoughts and feelings. Sebastian's significance resides in his symbolic function as Viola's thematic twin.

Sebastian and Olivia serve to illustrate the love theme quite well. Olivia has expressed her love; Sebastian takes his place as the practical, common sense complement to the loving aspect. His

soliloquy reflects his appreciation for the role of reason and prudent management in life. He praises Olivia for the latter.

Study Questions

1. Why is the garden an appropriate setting for this scene?
2. What does Sebastian try to come to terms with?
3. What does the rapidity of the love match prevent us from obtaining?
4. What gift has Olivia given Sebastian?
5. Whom does Sebastian wish to speak with?
6. Does he accept or reject Olivia's love?
7. What skill of Olivia's does Sebastian praise?
8. What plans has Olivia made?
9. Who has she brought to carry out those plans?
10. What is the key symbolic element of this scene?

Answers

1. It is appropriate because a wedding is about to take place.
2. Sebastian tries to come to terms with his good luck.
3. The rapidity of the love match prevents us from obtaining Sebastian's feelings about love.
4. Olivia gives Sebastian a pearl.
5. Sebastian wishes to speak with Antonio.
6. He accepts Olivia's love.
7. Sebastian praises Olivia's management of affairs in the house.
8. Olivia has planned a wedding ceremony.
9. She has brought a priest to tie the knot.
10. The key symbolic element is the twins.

Suggested Essay Topics

1. What is an "arranged marriage"? Do you know of anyone who was part of an arrangement? What motives may be involved? Compare an arranged marriage to the manner in which Sebastian and Olivia are brought together.

2. Consider the influence of "accident and flood of fortune" on Sebastian's success with Olivia. Is the marriage just good luck and is Sebastian taking advantage of an opportunity to marry up? Discuss Sebastian's attitude to Olivia in your essay.

SECTION SIX

Act V

Act V, Scene 1

Summary

This scene forms a conglomeration of previous elements in the play. We are before Olivia's house when it opens with Fabian and the Clown. Fabian is asking Feste to show him Malvolio's letter to Olivia, which he doesn't want to show him.

After this brief exchange, the Duke, Cesario, Curio, and other lords are on the scene. After inquiring of Feste and Fabian if they are connected to Olivia, the Duke recognizes one of them as the Clown. Upon being asked how he is, the Clown starts in with his wordplay. He answers ironically that, as far as his foes are concerned, he is better, and as far as his friends are concerned, he is worse. That makes no sense to the Duke, so he requests an explanation. The Clown's explanation holds that friends deceive, while enemies tell the cold truth. Once explained, the Duke likes the idea and tips him. The Clown wants more and gets another coin from the Duke. Before leaving to summon Olivia, the Clown requests yet another coin from the Duke.

Antonio and the officers then enter. Cesario recognizes Antonio as the man who stepped in on his fight with Sir Andrew. The Duke also recognizes Antonio from the time when he did courageous battle with one of his ships. An officer relates that he arrested Antonio while fighting in the street. Cesario hastens to his defense mentioning his help, though his speech quite perplexed him.

Antonio recounts how he saved Sebastian, inadvertently referring to Cesario, and offered his love and service to him. He exposed himself to danger for Sebastian's sake. Yet, Sebastian denied him when he intervened in the fight. Sebastian held back his purse, too.

Cesario wonders how that could be possible. He has been under the Duke's service since arriving in Illyria.

In walks Olivia asking the Duke how she can be of service to him. She takes Cesario for Sebastian. Olivia's speech thus baffles Cesario. Olivia repeats her rejection of the Duke. The Duke expresses his disappointment and adds a fierce note for emphasis. He retaliates by spiriting Cesario away, out of Olivia's sight. Cesario, supportive of the Duke, reveals his love for him.

Olivia calls for the priest to remind Cesario that they are married. She thinks that Cesario is afraid to admit the truth. The priest comes to substantiate the marital bond that exists between them (her and Sebastian). This proof convinces the Duke, who becomes angry with Cesario.

Sir Andrew, entering injured, calls for a doctor to attend him and Sir Toby. Sir Andrew lays the blame for this violence on Cesario. Cesario, of course, denies the charge. Sir Andrew was set on him by Sir Toby. Sir Toby enters limping and requests a doctor. Olivia orders him to bed.

Sebastian enters with an apology for the injuries he has produced. He was justified inasmuch as he acted in self-defense. The Duke notices the resemblance between him and Cesario, considering it an optical illusion. Sebastian is glad to see Antonio.

For the first time in the play, Sebastian speaks to Cesario. Cesario offers clear proof that he and Sebastian are related. The time is not right for Cesario to unmask, but he promises to bring Sebastian to where his woman's clothes are hidden.

Sebastian characterizes Olivia's mistake as natural since she was attracted to Cesario's masculine exterior.

Seeing a chance for his own happiness, the Duke shows interest in Cesario. Cesario accepts because she did, in fact, fall in love with him. The Duke wishes to see the Viola beneath the Cesario.

Olivia then requests to see Malvolio, at which point the Clown enters with his letter. Feste continues to ascribe madness to Malvolio. Irked by his unusual manner of reading the letter, Olivia asks Fabian to read it. The letter blames Olivia for the cruel joke that's been played on him. Though her love letter led him astray, he still kept his wits about him. He intends to broadcast the wrong she's done him. Olivia requests to see him.

The Duke proposes to Viola.

Malvolio enters chastising Olivia. She need only read her letter for the proof. Malvolio asked what possessed her to stoop to such a wicked scheme. Olivia recognizes the handwriting as Maria's and assures Malvolio that he will get justice. Fabian confesses his and the others' wrongdoing. He attributes their actions to "some stubborn and uncourteous parts," character flaws in them. Now that the trick has been exposed, Malvolio vows revenge on all those involved. Olivia acknowledges the abuse he's suffered at her servants' hands.

The Duke desires that a solemn combination be made of their hearts at a propitious hour. The third couple to join the other two is Maria and Sir Toby. Sir Toby proposed to Maria as a reward for her cleverness.

Analysis

This is the last scene of the play, so Shakespeare must provide a sense of closure. The way the action wraps up determines the overall meaning of the play. The genre of comedy has already provided us with some sense of the play's message. The dizzying sequence of interludes mirrors the festive form of the previous acts and gives the impression of a large holiday gathering. This scene is a fitting conglomeration of the play's elements—all the more satisfying because it resolves previous misunderstandings and complications. It ends in a happy "combination" of three couples. Even Malvolio is presented with some consolation from Olivia.

The Clown's irreverence toward the Duke is entirely in character. He is a wit to the very end. The Duke, pleased with his foolery, tips him twice before he goes off to get Olivia.

Antonio is necessary as a catalyst to the recognition scene. Having already raised hope of Sebastian's existence for Cesario, in this scene, Antonio dramatizes the duality of character. He speaks to Cesario as though he were Sebastian, which astonishes Cesario. The twins look alike, but they are not the same person. Antonio's previous dealings have been with Sebastian.

When Olivia enters, the Duke speaks the last words of love to her that he will ever speak. She has remained steadfast in her rejection. He acknowledges how futile his passion has been.

The confusion over mistaken identities continues a bit longer as Cesario prepares to leave with Orsino. Olivia speaks to Cesario as though he were her husband. This causes more astonishment for the Duke and Cesario—clarification has not yet come. The priest adds to the confusion by confirming the marriage ceremony between Sebastian and Olivia.

Happily the moment of recognition and resolution comes when Sebastian himself enters hard on the heels of Sir Andrew and Sir Toby. The twins, now together for the first time in the play, face each other and make their relationship clear. They are brother and sister. This clarification paves the way for the pairing of Viola and the Duke: "You shall from this time be/Your master's mistress." Critics offer numerous opinions on this ending. Alexander Leggat affirms that the play embodies the theme of love: "The ending takes little account of the reasons for particular attachments; it is, on the contrary, a generalized image of love." The pairings make up a formal design, which, in turn, illustrates the theme.

The cruel scheme against Malvolio is also laid bare in this scene. Fabian reads Malvolio's letter in which he accuses Olivia of abuse. Knowing herself innocent, Olivia requests to see Malvolio. When Malvolio comes, Olivia has a chance to vindicate herself and assign the blame to Maria where it belongs, for she composed the letter. Once again, this resolution, which may perhaps be cathartic for Malvolio, becomes a perverse reflection of the resolution of the love plot. Olivia tries to console him with the prospect of justice being served, while Malvolio, more harshly, thirsts for revenge.

Feste ends the play with a song, which unlike previous examples, has a looser connection to the action. The fact that the rain comes down every day has a bearing on their lives and activities. By referring to life's stages and natural imagery, he places the action in a larger, more ambiguous context. The song tells us how we are to take all the confusion and how we are to react to it. We shouldn't take troubles too seriously; life works itself out. The song is nonetheless open to interpretation. One critic has said of it that it is just "whistling in the dark."

Study Questions

1. Whose letter does Feste refuse to show Fabian?

2. With what disparaging term does the Clown refer to himself and Fabian?

3. Whom does Antonio think Cesario is?

4. Why does Olivia call in the priest?

5. What has happened to Sir Andrew?

6. What does Sebastian's presence signal?

7. Whom does Malvolio cast blame on in his letter?

8. With Olivia and Sebastian being the first couple, who make up the second couple?

9. Who make up the third pairing?

10. What satisfaction does Malvolio want for the trick?

Answers

1. Feste refuses to show Malvolio's letter.

2. The Clown refers to Fabian and himself as Olivia's "trappings."

3. Antonio thinks Cesario is Sebastian.

4. Olivia calls in the priest to verify her marriage to Sebastian.

5. Sir Andrew has been injured by Sebastian.

6. Sebastian's presence signals the resolution of the mistaken identity plot.

7. Malvolio casts blame on Olivia.

8. The second couple consists of the Duke and Viola.

9. Sir Toby and Maria make up the third couple.

10. Malvolio desires revenge on all his malefactors.

Suggested Essay Topics

1. Explain Antonio's function in the play. Is he a minor or major character? Does he clarify or interpret what is going on with the twins? Does he oppose or support the twins?

2. Isolate the methods that Shakespeare uses to establish and reveal character. It would probably be best to do a character study of one particular character. Are the actions of the characters properly motivated and consistent?

Sample Analytical Paper Topics

The following paper topics are designed to test your under-standing of the play as a whole and to analyze important themes and literary devices. Following each question is a sample outline to help you get started.

Topic #1

It is obvious that the play's tapestry contains more than a single plot. Write an essay analyzing the way in which the comic plot involving Malvolio becomes a perverse reflection of the love plot involving Orsino and Olivia. Discuss Cesario's role as go-between for the Duke.

Outline

I. Thesis Statement: *The comic plot involving Malvolio becomes a perverse reflection of the romantic plot involving Olivia and the Duke.*

II. Explain the romantic plot.

    A. An aristocratic man falls in love with a countess.

        1. The Duke has seen Olivia and desires union with her.

        2. He initially expresses the depth of his feeling in po-etic lines.

    B. Cesario acts as a go-between for the Duke.

        1. Cesario forms a practical complement to the Duke's romantic behavior.

      2.   Cesario woos Olivia on the Duke's behalf.

   C. Olivia rejects the Duke's love.

      1.   Olivia says that she cannot love the Duke while she mourns her brother's death.

      2.   Olivia, rather, falls in love with Cesario.

III. Explain the comic plot.

   A. Maria plots to gull Malvolio.

      1.   There is no genuine source for Malvolio's love; it's the result of a scheme.

      2.   The letter left by Maria is falsified.

   B. Malvolio picks up and reads a falsified letter.

      1.   The letter seems to be in Olivia's hand.

      2.   It commands him to adopt peculiar behaviors.

   C. Malvolio proceeds under the influence of a devious trick.

      1.   Malvolio thinks Olivia is in love with him.

      2.   Malvolio approaches Olivia in yellow stockings and cross-gartered.

IV. Malvolio's love is a perversion of the Duke's and Olivia's.

   A. Malvolio's love is an artificial fantasy—put stress on the "artificial."

      1.   Malvolio loves on the basis of a letter and a readiness in his own mind.

      2.   Malvolio's love has no possibility of being realized because Olivia has no intention of loving him.

   B. Orsino, by contrast, is truly in love with Olivia.

      1.   Orsino's feelings have a genuine source.

      2.   Orsino is truly involved in an effort to court a woman.

      3.   Ideally, he could possibly achieve Olivia.

   C. Malvolio winds up humiliated.

      1.   Malvolio isolates himself with a sense of being abused.

    2.   Rather than being an accepted lover, Malvolio winds up wronged and humiliated.

V.   Conclusion: To the extent that the schemers are cruel, Malvolio's love for Olivia is perverse. Love cannot thrive in an atmosphere of ill will.

Topic # 2

Many playwrights have dealt with the theme of love. It's a theme that carries so much interest because of the power it wields in peoples' lives. Write an essay that explores Shakespeare's treatment of the theme of love in *Twelfth Night.*

Outline

I.   Thesis Statement: *The formal design of* Twelfth Night *illustrates the theme of love as having two key aspects, "loving" and maintaining the relationship.*

II.   The aspect of "loving" as embodied in the play

    A.   Define the concept of "loving."

        1.   The Duke serves as an example of the true lover.

        2.   The Duke places Olivia on a pedestal.

    B.   Olivia falls in love with Cesario.

        1.   Just as the Duke loved Olivia upon seeing her, so Olivia loves Cesario when they meet.

        2.   Olivia pours forth poetic feeling for Cesario.

    C.   Both Orsino and Olivia are rejected in their loving.

        1.   Olivia rejects the love of the Duke.

        2.   Cesario rejects Olivia's love.

III.   Cesario represents the practical aspect of love that sustains a relationship.

    A.   Cesario goes to work for the Duke.

        1.   Cesario's speech shows that he understands the need to be realistic and practical.

      2.   Cesario diligently attempts to woo Olivia for the Duke.

B.   Cesario does not give himself over to sentiment.

      1.   Cesario does not fall in love and utter love speeches.

      2.   Cesario is a man of action, not of words.

C.   Cesario has a twin brother.

      1.   Cesario's twin brother, Sebastian, will prove a similar complement to Olivia.

      2.   Olivia's love is similar to the Duke's in its romantic nature.

IV. The two aspects of love are brought together in the final harmony of the play.

A.   Sebastian enters Illyria.

      1.   Sebastian is puzzled over Olivia's immediate affection for him.

      2.   The two lovers can achieve their other halves because Sebastian joins Viola.

B.   Cesario reveals his true female identity.

      1.   Olivia and Sebastian have married; Cesario is not a man.

      2.   The Duke can propose to Viola upon learning of Olivia's marriage.

C.   The couples of the love plot complement each other perfectly.

      1.   Cesario is the practical aspect that sustains the love which Orsino embodies.

      2.   Sebastian, like his sister, represents the practical aspect for Olivia's amalgam of love feeling.

V.   Conclusion: Looking at a theme in an abstract sort of way, as here with love, requires that the play be seen quite like a static work of art. Characters thus become more like poetic symbols than real, dynamic personalities.

Topic # 3

The festive atmosphere is so much a part of this play that it should be considered to gain a deeper understanding. Sir Toby, as the "lord of misrule," is the master of ceremonies and surely keeps the party going. Write an essay that explores the function of the foolery and fun within the play.

Outline

I.   Thesis Statement: *Shakespeare weaves in a festive atmosphere that enhances the enjoyment of the love plot.*

II. Define the festive atmosphere.

    A. The title *Twelfth Night* indicates a holiday and day of revelry.

        1. Tradition places a "lord of misrule" in charge of the fun in this play.

        2. The holiday includes eating, drinking, and entertainment.

    B. Sir Toby handles the merriment quite well.

        1. Sir Toby and Sir Andrew eat and drink for diversion.

        2. Sir Toby instigates a fight that provides high-spirited entertainment.

    C. The Clown plays a remarkable role in the festivities.

        1. The Clown is a jester who is clever at wordplay.

        2. The Clown sings for the Duke and the other characters.

III. The saturnalia is absorbed in the action of the play.

    A. The gulling of Malvolio as an example of high jinks

        1. Sir Toby approves of the way Maria orchestrates the scheme.

        2. The spectators take eerie pleasure in Malvolio's humiliation.

    B. Imagery underscores the awareness of a holiday

    1.   Sir Toby uses dance images in a conversation with Sir Andrew.

    2.   Sir Toby refers to wines and has a reputation for being a drunk.

C. Feste's role in the festive design

    1.   He impersonates Sir Topas when speaking with Malvolio.

    2.   Feste and Cesario have a meeting of the minds in their conversation.

IV. The intersection of the festive element and the love theme

A. Sir Andrew as one of Sir Toby's men has a mock duel with Cesario.

    1.   Sir Toby suggests that a show of valor will entice Olivia.

    2.   Sir Andrew is egged on to confront Cesario.

B. The content of the Clown's songs relates to the theme of love.

    1.   The first song Feste sings deals with true love.

    2.   Feste also sings a song that expresses Orsino's frustrated love.

C. The last act consists in a dizzying array of interludes.

    1.   The act has the semblance of a large party with all the characters coming together to share in the roistering.

    2.   Sir Toby marries Maria in recompense for her cleverness.

V. Conclusion: Love can thrive in almost any environment. But, perhaps an ambience that is full of fun and liveliness can best match the emotional high that being in love means for some.

SECTION EIGHT

Bibliography

Quotations of *Twelfth Night* are taken from the following edition:

Shakespeare, William. *Twelfth Night*, ed. Herschel Baker. New York: New American Library, 1965.

Other Sources:

Abrams, M.H. *A Glossary of Literary Terms.* New York: Holt, Rinehart and Winston, 1981.

Barber, C.L. *Shakespeare's Festive Comedy.* Princeton: Princeton University Press, 1959.

Berry, Ralph. *Shakespeare's Comedies.* Princeton: Princeton University Press, 1972.

Brown, John. R. *Shakespeare and His Comedies.* London: Methuen & Co., Ltd., 1957.

Charney, Maurice. *All of Shakespeare.* New York: Columbia University Press, 1993.

Frye, Northrop. *Anatomy of Criticism.* Princeton: Princeton University Press, 1957.

Gaylin, Willard. *Rediscovering Love.* New York: Viking Penguin, Inc., 1986.

Leggatt, Alexander. *Shakespeare's Comedy of Love.* London: Methuen & Co., Ltd., 1974.

Levin, Richard. *Love and Society in Shakespearean Comedy.* Newark: University of Delaware Press, 1985.

Randle, John. *Understanding Britain.* Oxford: Basil Blackwell Publisher, 1981.

Schultz, Harold J. *History of England.* New York: Harper & Row, 1980.

Swinden, Patrick. *An Introduction to Shakespeare's Comedies.* London: The Macmillan Press, Ltd., 1973.

Encyclopedias

Britannica. Volume 27. Chicago: Encyclopedia Britannica, 1993, pp. 253–262.

Parrot, Thomas Marc. "William Shakespeare." *Collier's Encyclopedia.* New York: P.F. Collier, 1992, pp. 631–636.

Smith, Hallet. "William Shakespeare." *Encyclopedia Americana.* Danbury: Grolier Incorporated, 1994, pp. 652–659.